Healing the Feminine
Your Path to Health and Wholeness

We live in a troubled world. In addition to the inner
anguish of emotional distress, we suffer from from addictions,
immune system disorders, and "heart disease." We are at war
with each other and within ourselves. Women are violâted.
The earth is raped. These problems have reached catastrophic
proportions, and unless we do something about them, we may
cease to exist.

Many of today's difficulties stem from a fundamental
imbalance in the core of our world. We have lost our ties with
Mother Nature, with Woman's Voice, and the feminine in our
nature. The feminine is suppressed, oppressed—abused.

Everyone suffers the consequences of society's devaluation of the feminine. Men disown feelings. Females struggle
with depression and low self-esteem; we suffer from eating
disorders, co-dependency, all the catchwords of addiction.
These difficulties are symptoms. The feminine is crying out for
attention, asking to be healed.

Healing the Feminine is a creative process—an inner journey. Using her own experiences and those of clients, Dr.
Lesley Irene Shore takes the reader on a healing journey into
disowned and dispossessed parts of the psyche. Women learn
to nurture their bodies, live in harmony with inner rhythms,
and feel "good" about themselves.

About the Author

Lesley Irene Shore, Ph.D. is a counseling psychologist with over 25 years of varied experience. In addition to working in counseling centers, clinics, and hospitals, she has also held academic appointments at Harvard Medical School and the Massachusetts School for Professional Psychology. Dr. Shore now practices on Harmony Farm in Medfield, Massachusetts, and is the author of *Tending Inner Gardens: The Healing Art of Feminist Psychotherapy*.

To Write to the Author

If you wish to contact the author or would like more information about this book, please write to the author in care of Llewellyn Worldwide, and we will forward your request. Both the author and publisher appreciate hearing from you and learning of your enjoyment of this book and how it has helped you. Llewellyn Worldwide cannot guarantee that every letter written to the author can be answered, but all will be forwarded. Please write to:

Dr. Lesley Irene Shore
℅ Llewellyn Worldwide
P.O. Box 64383-667, St. Paul, MN 55164-0383, U.S.A.
Please enclose a self-addressed, stamped envelope for reply,
or $1.00 to cover costs
If outside the U.S.A., enclose international postal reply coupon.

Free Catalog from Llewellyn

For more than 90 years Llewellyn has brought its readers knowledge in the fields of metaphysics and human potential. Learn about the newest books in spiritual guidance, natural healing, astrology, occult philosophy and more. Enjoy book reviews, new age articles, a calendar of events, plus current advertised products and services. To get your free copy of *Llewellyn's New Worlds of Mind and Spirit*, send your name and address to:

Llewellyn's New Worlds of Mind and Spirit
P.O. Box 64383-667, St. Paul, MN 55164-0383, U.S.A.

To Cheryl
Listen to the
voices inside

Healing the Feminine

Reclaiming Woman's Voice

by
Lesley Irene Shore, Ph.D.

Lesley Irene Shore

1995
Llewellyn Publications
St. Paul, Minnesota 55164-0383, U.S.A.

FIRST EDITION, 1992
SECOND EDITION
First Printing, 1995
formerly published as *Reclaiming Woman's Voice*

Cover art by Katherine Ace
Cover design by Anne Marie Garrison

Library of Congress Cataloging-in-Publication Data
Shore, Lesley Irene.
        Healing the feminine : reclaiming woman's voice / by
    Lesley Irene Shore. — 2nd ed.
            p.   cm.
        Rev. ed. of: Reclaiming woman's voice. 1st ed. 1992.
        Includes bibliographical references and index.
        ISBN 1-56718-667-X
        1. Women — Psychology. 2. Femininity (Psychology)
    3. Self-actualization (Psychology) I. Shore, Lesley Irene.
    Reclaiming woman's voice. II. Title.
    HQ1206.S486   1994
    155.3'33 — dc20   94-29650

Llewellyn Publications
A Division of Llewellyn Worldwide, Ltd.
P.O. Box 64383, St. Paul, MN 55164-0383

To
Grandmother

ABOUT MY CLIENTS

I'm indebted to my clients. While trusting me, initially a stranger, with their deepest feelings, they had the courage to take the inner journey. By sharing their experiences, they taught me a great deal of the material in this book. I've included some of their stories, but have protected their identities by changing their names.

ACKNOWLEDGEMENTS

How can I ever thank all the people who have helped bring this book into being? There are too many to list, for every person who touched my life is part of my growth. As I've called upon all of my life's experiences in writing this book, granting recognition to each person would be a book in itself.

Having said all of the above, I do want to selectively mention a few special people who have been actively engaged in my writing process. This is my one opportunity to publicly acknowledge their contribution.

Special thanks are due to my readers: Priscilla Cogan, Maida Greenberg, Geri Reinhardt, Hanna Shore, Liesl Silverstone, Bill Tragakis, Michael Tragakis, and Tina VanDerwater. I probably would never have written this book without their loving support and constructive criticism. They each helped me become "a writer," for their faith in me and my writing gave me the nerve to keep searching for words to express what I was trying to say. I am especially indebted to Cilla for feeding my muse with reams of challenging comments and leading questions.

I'm grateful that Carl Weschcke had the vision to print this book. Thanks to him, I've enjoyed working with the many warm, caring, sensitive, human beings at Llewellyn. And while the entire staff has contributed, in one way or another, to the success of this book, I appreciate the recent efforts of Nancy Mostad, Lily Winter, Luann Wolfe, Lee Owens, Marilyn Matheny, and Lynne Menturweck.

I'd like to thank my husband, Bill Tragakis, for insisting upon his "crazy" idea of living on a farm. His vision changed both of our lives, and made Harmony Farm possible. I'm grateful for his loving presence in my life, and for standing steadily beside me throughout this complicated birthing.

I thank my children, Jim, Steve, and Mike, for giving me so many opportunities to grow, and for loving me even with my flaws.

And I thank my parents for the gift of my life, for their inner strength, and their constant love.

TABLE OF CONTENTS

Introduction

Several years have elapsed since I first wrote this book. Much has changed during this time, but the dynamics this book explores are even more pertinent today.

Despite continued movement toward political and economic parity, the "female problem" hasn't gone away. Women climb corporate ladders and pursue higher education, yet we're still plagued by depression and low self-esteem.

Young girls know opportunities are available to them as well as their male peers. Nevertheless, recent research (Brown & Gilligan, 1992) shows that girls' self-esteem drops dramatically as they approach adolescence. And despite all that has been written about eating disorders, this predominantly female symptom is increasing, rather than decreasing. Moreover, girls are developing eating disorders at younger ages.

"Something" continues to be very, very wrong.

I'll be exploring the roots of these difficulties in the following pages, showing you that we still live in an imbalanced world, a world which values the masculine at the expense of the feminine. Everyone, both male and female, suffers the consequences of this societal imbalance. We've *all* been abusing the feminine.

And so I invite you to take a healing journey—a journey of healing the feminine. Our journey will take us into dissociated parts of the psyche, the unconscious. This uncharted territory is abandoned land. It is where Woman's Voice may be found.

Woman's Voice is the voice of the feminine—a dissociated, suppressed, and neglected aspect of our mechanistic world. Her voice is within each person, but separated off, shunted aside, shut away, and hidden. Woman's Voice is crying inside all of us, asking to be healed.

As we take this healing journey, I'll be sharing my experiences—my own inner journey as well as those of my clients. You may notice "something" resonating inside you. A neglected, disowned, dispossessed part of you may call out, asking to be heard.

I encourage you to listen to your "something"—travel inside yourself, locate this missing aspect, hear what "it" has to say. And as you name it, value it, and connect with it, something else will begin to happen. *Healing the Feminine* has a rippling effect that can transform your life.

Let the healing begin!

Voices

Harmony Farm

I live on Harmony Farm, the name we gave to our home in anticipation of relationships that would unfold. We built our house amidst wild woods and open fields, surrounded by untamed life, both animal and vegetable. Here we garden organically, raise chickens and sheep, and work towards living in tune with nature.

There are no neatly manicured lawns on Harmony Farm. The house is nestled in a hollow created by undulating land. On one side of the house is a pine grove, with its aromatic carpet of reddish-brown pine needles. The sun rises from here, a welcome sight any time of the year. It sets to the west where our barn is visible through trees on the other side of the house, with fields, garden and sheep just beyond. Our days are marked by the movement of the sun appearing over the pines, traveling from one end of the house to the other, and then falling behind a hill above our field.

Tall oak trees rise up behind the house. They keep us in tune with the seasons, for they enter our home through large expanses of glass lining the south side. During summer their lush leaves provide shade, protecting and sheltering us from unwelcome heat. Fall is a time of transformation as their leaves become waves of moving color. Winter is signaled by shedding leaves, inviting the bright, warming rays of sunlight into our home. Each spring we rejoice as leaves expand and unfurl, renewing life.

Our "front yard" is a naturalistic array of herbs and wildflowers. My presence is evident here where soil had been laid barren and bare by bulldozers. I planted some favorite herbs and flowering plants, and once they set root invited Mother Nature to lend a helping hand. She was given a free rein, apparently delighting in displaying her ability to regenerate herself. Using plants I had given her, she set fruit, ripened seed, interspersed them amongst one another, and then sent birds from fields afar to drop some seed here, some fertilizer there. Only the most noxious of intruders was weeded out. The resulting effect is a medley of aromas, colors, textures, shapes and sizes—a living impressionistic painting.

My life is as rich and varied as the naturalistic setting surrounding my home. I weave my life with many threads. Each adds color. Each adds texture. My roles as wife, mother, friend, and daughter are some of the strands creating the fabric of my life. My professional life is a main thread, with the remarkable property of expanding and contracting to make room for the necessities of other threads. A nubby thread made of many strands, my career as psychologist and psychotherapist intertwines with healer, nurturer and gardener, creating a naturally evolving whole tapestry. The threads go back to England.

When I was young I lived in England, famous for lush lawns and "herbaceous borders" filled with lupines, delphiniums, poppies, peonies, bluebells. Fog and rain brought abundant moisture, enabling colorful carpets to flourish practically year round. During cold,

damp, gloomy winters, green warmed my chilled heart.
In summer she brought cooling breezes that refreshed
the soul.

I remember one warm summer day when I was
about eight. School was in session, and the classroom
was stifling. Our teacher decided to take us outside to a
large weeping willow tree growing in a nearby grassy
area. Class was held underneath the great wide
branches of this tree. And as the branches touched the
ground in a large circle, we were surrounded by green.
Inside this leafy, enveloping, womb-like space was a
cool comfortable cozy place. We learned many things
that day, sitting encircled in the arms of this tree.

Listening to my teacher, I heard the wind whispering secrets to the surrounding branches. The
branches waved to the breeze in a sign language I did
not understand, but could feel music in the words. The
sunlight, not to be left out of this playful mood, danced
between the long tapered leaves, creating patterns of
moving light. The shadowy leafy reflections were
touched with green. Mesmerized by their movements I
wished to be able to dance with them, hold their hands
in mine, join the threads of our lives more visibly together.

While gray clouds hovered over my childhood, I
was also touched by green. There were dense forests
where we went mushrooming and played hide and
seek. When I crawled inside the trunk of an old tree,
exploring the safety of this protected hiding place, I
discovered soft, lush moss cushioning every move. Cra-
dled inside the tree, comforted by moss, all was safe
and still, peaceful and quiet.

When I was ten my family traveled across the

ocean, moved to a strange land. Transplanted into new soil, I took a while adjusting to the alien environment. After re-setting roots, my teenage years filled with typical adolescent preoccupations. Green moved further into the background.

In college I knew that something was troubling me. I wrote poignant papers decrying the separations and differentiations characteristic of our society. The ideas of Oriental philosophy resonated with something in me—their valuing the whole as well as the parts, the forces that intertwine as well as the separations and distinctions, the interdependence of opposites.

College was followed by graduate school. This time the classroom was in New York City, where there were no weeping willow trees. The oppressive gray of winter and the stultifying heat of summer could not be tempered by green. In those misty mornings of missing green, I pined away for the resplendent forests of my youth.

My early years of young adulthood were spent dappled by green as I moved back and forth from city to suburb to city to suburb, grappling to grow through developmental tasks imposed by my years. The green times were always the best times, full of color and rich with possibility. Green continued beckoning, calling my name, until I moved to the land we named Harmony Farm.

Little did I know how much my life would be influenced by living on Harmony Farm. Until I moved here I had been haunted by the sense that "something" was missing. I was always searching for something, yearning for something, but never quite knowing what I was looking for.

I spent many years yearning for the right man to come into my life. My imagination struggled to express itself in fantasies of meeting, finding, and being with a man in a close, loving, whole way. During adolescence I consumed romantic novels which further fed this fantasy of fulfillment with a man. When I married my husband I knew he was that right man. Yet, "something" was missing.

I looked to food, perhaps this would be that something to take in, that something I was yearning after. And so I focused on finding the right food, becoming an expert on health and nutrition, feeding my family healthy food. While there were benefits to my altered consumption, I kept consuming and consuming. Nothing quite satisfied. Nothing took away that hunger, that yearning.

Others saw me as capable and competent. And I was capable and competent. Yet, "something" was missing. So I completed one degree after another, hoping I might ultimately feel whole, find that sense of completeness I was apparently searching for. A Ph.D. wasn't the solution. "Something" was missing.

There were also jobs—one good job after another, fancy titles one after another—each time gaining more experience—growing, helping others grow. And even though I was able to help people and teach others the tools of my helping profession, I was still searching.

After we moved to Harmony Farm some strange things began happening. I had difficulty leaving, going to work. There was a sense of something forgotten, something left behind, nagging, calling me back. I found many excuses to return to check the woodburning stove, the door. Going away for vacation was similarly difficult, and my children always joked as we traveled down the driveway, reminding me to return and look for that forgotten piece.

Nature had always beckoned, and I hadn't heard her calling. I had always known that I loved being around growing things, always had a few house plants to talk to and, whenever possible, a garden to tend. When I moved to Harmony Farm I began hearing her differently. I heard Her voice.

I began planting some lavender here, a peony there, and wanted lilacs blooming everywhere. There was no end to my enthusiasm, my energy, my delight. I felt as if I had finally found home, wandering around our gardens, watching over them, taking care of them. Whenever possible, I went barefoot, delighting in the sensations as my feet made contact with soft damp earth. It was as if we communicated, that earth and I. Her voice whispered in my ear and I bent to do Her task.

During months when I was unable to garden, the outdoors still beckoned. I took long, contemplative walks. Until then my life had been focused on people, on activity, speed. I led a fast paced life, racing down ski slopes, running to keep appointments, rushing to finish one diploma after another. Yet, when I moved to Harmony Farm I began taking walks. I found myself delighting in the process of slowly putting one foot in front of the other again and again.

It was on these walks that "something" started shifting inside. As one foot moved in front of the other, my attention traveled inward. I became absorbed inside myself. Sometimes I focused on a problem that was troubling me at the time. My mind circled around it—getting to know it, learning about it from one perspective then another. I didn't think about the problem. It evolved in my mind, quietly turning round and around, giving me a chance to fully explore it.

At other times, I found myself taken with a branch, a bird. Something from nature reached out, grabbed hold of me, entered my being. It happened without my being aware it was happening.

My mind was free to roam and wander. As my feet found their way along their path, my thoughts also wandered, roamed down inner trails, weaving in and out. It was my time with myself—time to reflect, to ponder, to travel within, to journey.

My walks took me along horsetrails and cart roads through our property and adjoining land. I enjoyed walking by myself, exploring one trail then another, getting the lay of the land. There were no maps to guide my way, only the joy of discovery.

And there was much to discover. Weaving my way along the paths, feeling my way around the area's nooks and crannies, I began discovering the pleasure in quiet, the peace in stillness. I learned that there is much to hear in stillness, much to see if one slows down one's pace.

I began hearing birds, tuning in to their songs. They sang to me as I walked along the trails. I began hearing the colors of the leaves, tasting the smell of the air, feeling the changing seasons. My senses came alive in new and different ways.

I heard Woman's Voice. Not actually hearing a voice, but feeling it in that woman's place of knowing, that woman's way of knowing—in the center of my being. I opened my self to Her. She spoke to me in the still times, the silent times, the quiet times.

She spoke to me as one season moved into another. She showed me her cycles—seasonal cycles, life cycles, ripples in the wind—flowing cycles, always moving, flowing into each other in an endless spiral of becoming. She taught me about interrelationships—how she weaves a whole with parts, each part contributing to the whole, each part affected by the whole. A ripple, somewhere, is felt everywhere.

And as I began feeling these ripples, something shifted and changed inside me. It was a subtle, subterranean metamorphosis. I never knew it was happening. All I knew was that I felt different. "Something" had shifted.

There were times when I felt whole and complete. These times were usually when I was outside, with nature—weeding, walking, planting. Whenever I was with Her I felt different—more content, more serene. That sense of searching for something missing faded into the background. I developed a different relationship within myself and with my body. I began hearing my inner voice and connecting with the feminine.

Nature guided me into myself, towards the feminine. She helped me connect with the missing aspects of my self, the lost part. My roots grew into my center, found fertile ground. I became myself.

These changes reverberated throughout my life. I was leading a different lifestyle—a lifestyle that grew out of my relationship with the earth, with the seasons, out of my rootedness in my self. I was sensing and feeling differently, and wanted to make sense out of these experiences, understand them.

And so I continued searching—searching through

books about women, about nature, about women and nature. And I continued listening closely to clients as they talked about their struggles, their difficulties, their dilemmas. Once I became grounded in my self, firmly planted in the earth, I began branching out, finding new ways of being, new ways of being with others.

Wanting to expose all my clients to the healing influence of nature, I left other professional positions and established a full-time private practice on Harmony Farm. I aimed to create a healing therapy, one that imitates nature's healing aspect, creates inner balance where there has been imbalance. My therapy became less analytic and mechanistic, more natural and connected. My hearing changed. I listened in new ways.

The female voices in my office spoke of feeling sad and heavy, a heaviness they couldn't throw off by dint of will or determination. And while this internal sense of feeling oppressed was sometimes matched by an awareness of an oppressive force in the form of society, husband, or event in their lives, this wasn't always the case. They were often unable to identify the origins of their malaise.

Listening to their struggles, I heard similar themes. They were sad, lonely, oppressed and empty themes. Their voices spoke of wanting, of yearning, of searching. They vividly described wanting more from their husbands, their children, their lovers or their parents. They felt "empty inside." Even though some women identified the emptiness as "a hole," or "a bottomless pit," many were unable to define their emptiness. Others could only becry a nothingness inside.

While many women want something for inside, they find what is outside to be wanting.

My female clients spoke of shame. They blamed themselves for their inability to find whatever it was they were searching for. They felt inadequate—not good enough or lacking in an essential characteristic. Their voices echoed one another, harmonizing into a single song about themselves.

And as I walked with nature, I heard my clients singing their blues. I walked rhythmically, listening to the sounds of their voices, hearing their intensity, their timbre, their overtones, their undertones. They sang with one voice—a hollow voice, filled with shame, empty. It was a soulful song.

And I began hearing the melody behind their words, the music in their words, their rhythm. I was weaving the pieces together, hearing the missing behind the words. Recalling my earlier years of searching, I understood there was a reason for my search. Something had been missing. Something had been lost. And I began recognizing what it was. It had to do with the feminine.

These lost feelings were part of my inheritance, part of the inheritance of men and women. This was the music behind my client's words—the missing piece.

We have lost our ties with Mother Nature, with Woman's Voice, with the feminine. We've been missing our connection with nature's cycles, with the feminine in our nature. Harmony Farm helped me locate that missing piece. Now I help others take *their* journey.

Female Voices

The concepts of masculine and feminine are ways of thinking about our world and our selves. As opposite ends of a continuum, opposite sides of the same coin, they balance and complement each other. Together they create a whole.

Archaeological and mythological evidence suggests that the feminine once had a powerful voice (Campbell, 1980; Gimbutas, 1982, 1989; Stone, 1976; Walker, 1983). Our forebearers paid homage to a mother earth goddess, a supreme female deity who ruled over all living things as well as subordinate gods and goddesses. During this peaceful time, which traces back to about 25,000 B.C., harmony between masculine and feminine was reflected in the relationships between men and women. Their roles complemented one another. It was an egalitarian society where women and nature were respected.

This social order changed somewhere between five and ten thousand years ago. A transition took place from a world view that emphasized the sacredness of an immanent earth mother goddess, to one that worships a transcendent heavenly father god. According to a number of scholars (French, 1985; Stone, 1976), this transition occasioned major social changes which resulted in the subjugation of women and nature.

We now live in an overly masculine world—a world created in His image, ruled over by a male god with a masculine view of the universe, structured according to power. It's an unbalanced world, with the masculine way of being overvalued and the feminine undervalued. Woman's Voice, the voice of the feminine, is suppressed. We've lost Her voice.

Our either/or society values separations and distinctions rather than wholes and relationships. It speaks with Man's Voice, the voice of the masculine— associated with the metaphor of science, of control, of power, of the machine. Value is placed on what is logical, rational, predictable and controllable. These metaphors are the ruling metaphors, the underlying mythology of our culture. They structure the shape of our cultural experience—the forms of our experiences and the meanings behind them. In this society relationships are structured around issues of power and control, rather than cooperation and mutuality.

Our society perpetuates disconnection—not out of necessity, but out of the prevailing ethos that permeates the culture. Valuing only the objectivity of science, we've become distrustful of that other way of knowing—the knowing in the heart, in the gut, in the essence of our being—the feminine way of knowing that is an inner knowing—a sensing, an intuitive tuning into a dimension of knowledge that is difficult to describe let alone measure or quantify. We've been closing ourselves off from this aspect of our selves—the side that's considered more connected, more intertwined, more feeling, more feminine. This part is disowned—relegated to the land of the dispossessed, the unconscious.

We all suffer the consequences of society's worship of the masculine and repression of the feminine. While we may try to separate from the feminine inside ourselves, we are inherently whole, feeling people with many aspects to our selves and our being. We seek balance. And we cannot totally disown that which is part of the self, the feminine. She raises Her voice, attempts to be heard, seeks to be reunited with the self. We struggle internally, battling with Her, trying to suppress this essential aspect of ourselves.

Both men and women struggle with the feminine inside their selves. While males disown their softer, feeling, intuitive, more feminine side, females face a complicated situation. As the conceptual inventions of masculine and feminine are confused with gender, females are identified with the feminine. We are expected to express the feminine.

Females are placed in a double-bind, no-win situation. In order to identify with the feminine, we must incorporate something that is devalued by society into our sense of ourselves. There is something then inherently wrong with us. This no-win situation has far-reaching psychological consequences for females. And while both men and women pay a price for society's devaluation of the feminine, this book will primarily explore the effects on women.

Over the years I've seen many clients. They are each unique and have their own form of difficulty. But while they have different symptoms, the underlying roots of their problems often lie in uneven development—emotional consequences of living in an imbalanced world. When they come to see me I listen to their words, and hear their voices.

Upon entering my office female clients notice the flowering plants, comment on their vibrant color, and marvel at their beauty. They are sending out their antennae, getting a feel for the place, trying to sense how safe it will be—whether or not they'll be able to speak about their difficulties, and whether I'll be able to hear their words, tune into their music. They are searching for someone to help heal wounds—wounds they know are there, but for which they have no name. Once inside my office they look around, getting the lay of the land, looking for a place to sit, wondering what might be expected of them. Sensing their uncertainty, I generally indicate where I sit, and invite them to either sit in the other large reclining chair, on the couch, or wherever they would be more comfortable. After another hesitating moment, they pick a place.

Having settled in a seat, they wonder how to begin. At first I gently encourage them by asking questions, inquiring into the nature of their difficulties. They start talking about feelings—their anxiety, their sadness, their sense of despair. The dam breaks. They're flooded with feelings which come spilling out, one after another, a torrent of feelings pouring forth—feelings about themselves, their lack of confidence, their insecurities, their inadequacies—feelings about a husband, a boyfriend, a lover, or lack of husband, boyfriend or lover—feelings about children or lack of children—feelings about their families. They yearn for closeness.

Talking about feelings, they say that they feel something is wrong with them, not quite right. All this has been going on such a long time, and doesn't seem to end. They just can't stop feeling depressed, or anxious, whichever it is. It isn't as if they haven't tried. Often they've talked with friends, read self-help books, listened to discussions on talk shows. And they still feel the same. Nothing has changed. They're still who they are, and haven't been able to feel differently.

Then they talk about people—their connections, their relationships. They describe their efforts to please—their concern lest someone important, or unimportant, become displeased with them. They care about the people in their lives—worry about their feelings, focus on their feelings, never want them to hurt.

Despite all this caring concern, they're never appreciated. Nobody *really* cares about them, loves them. They feel alone and unloved. And all they want is love, someone to care about them.

If I'm not careful, my female clients focus on what other people need, trying to ascertain how to better meet those needs, hoping they might then get what they are wanting for themselves. They describe these people to me in great detail, hoping I will shed some light on how they might better go about the business of pleasing them. I must make sure that I don't fall into the trap of analyzing these other people. My goal is to lead clients out of the entangled webs that threaten to strangle the life out of them.

Female clients often look to me for a prescription. They're so used to being told what to do, to meeting someone else's expectations, that they are ready to follow mine. They are quick to sense any suggestion I may have for them, often reading between my lines, hearing one where none exists. When I don't offer one, they're initially pleasantly surprised, then lost, not quite sure what to do next.

Listening to my female clients, I hear them flowing from one topic to another, following the thread of a feeling as it leads from one association to another. There are curves to their sentences as they weave in, out, and around an area of concern. Their thoughts don't always follow straight lines, but roam around, associating, seemingly in circles, escalating circles that reach further, moving ahead in arcs and waves. My female clients deal with wholes—whole feelings, whole experiences. They pull together, seeing connections, forming relationships, focusing on the relationships. And they look to connect with me.

When its time to leave my female clients gather themselves together, basking in the warmth, hesitant to have it abruptly end. Some offer to take out their check book, trying to further delay the process of extricating themselves from the chair. Once they manage to stand on their own two feet, they again pause, hesitate, and look at me. I sense them wanting to touch, embrace, feel human connection before tearing themselves asunder. On their way out they may notice the flowers.

I too look at the flowers, and then allow my mind to go blank. I'm clearing my mind, shifting, making space. Having found that I need time between appointments to transition from one person to another, I allow time for these shifts.

This space gives me time to contemplate my clients' dilemmas. Many of their difficulties stem from issues with the feminine. Society's pervasive, insidious influence cannot be avoided. Even when born into the best of families where she is valued and loved, a female is identified with the feminine. And this part of her is considered unacceptable, not good enough, bad.

Most women incorporate society's attitude towards the feminine. We devalue our selves. Despite external achievements and accomplishments, we have inner feelings of worthlessness and inadequacy. Our sense of worth is not tied to a realistic appraisal of our strengths and weaknesses. We don't feel "good enough."

Most women are caught in a trap. While we're generally discouraged from developing the masculine side of our selves, we're also unable to become rooted in the feminine. Without either the masculine or the feminine, there is no inner anchor to stabilize our journey through life. And instead of floundering or feeling lost, we send our roots outside our selves and look to become rooted in something of value—the masculine of society, or of a man. Other people become our anchors.

Living in a mechanistic, masculine dominated society, women are given the hidden, or not so hidden, message that we must separate from our basic nature. Logical, rational, reasoning is revered. Intuition is not respected. People aim to talk in straight lines, and women are accused of "talking in circles." Feelings are to be avoided, and yet women are seen as the repository of all feeling states. And while women are oriented towards caring about relationships and connections, society's scientific mentality commands that we be able to disconnect and "look at things objectively."

Faced with these dilemmas many women disconnect from the central aspect of their selves—the feminine. Our growth is stunted, shunted away from the earth within. We no longer hear Her voice.

Lost Voice

Masculine and feminine come together in the act of creation. A child is born. Birth is marked by a hearty cry, welcoming air into lungs, celebrating her first independent breath, the breath of life. With this breath she separates from her mother, from her origins, her roots. It is her first separation.

She experiments with using her breath, filling lungs with air, allowing it to rush through vocal cords, releasing sound along with air. Time and time again this action is repeated, perfecting the perfect breath, the open throated lusty cry, the expression of rage at being cut adrift from her mother. She begins to find Her voice.

The breath of air stirs her into activity. She starts exploring life, testing it out. Training goes on outside awareness.

She soon senses that there's something "bad" inside herself. She starts distrusting this something, stops listening to Her, begins hiding from Her. She learns not to trust what she feels. She hides the feelings, stops listening to them, stops talking about them. It doesn't take long. She loses Her voice.

She hides the feminine inside herself by closing Her off, shunting Her aside—away from her self. She pretends She isn't there. Soon she forgets where She is.

She's lost.

She's lost inside her self, crying out, waiting.

Dis-Sociation

Untitled

Names are important. They identify who we are, give us an identity. Even my dog has a name and knows to come when she's called, most of the time. However, married women lose their names, their titles. This is one of the ways society disempowers women, keeps them in their place.

A woman's identity is determined by her marital status, the condition of whether she is with or without a man, her relationship with him. Unlike a man who is considered to be "Mr." regardless of his marital status, a woman's identity changes when she gets married. She converts from "Miss" to "Mrs." This is society's method of categorizing women.

When the Ms. became an option, most married women continued to go by the Mrs., especially those who had changed their surname. It didn't make sense for them to use Ms. instead of Mrs. The damage had been done. And while many single women do opt to use Ms., this title has merely replaced the Miss and has, unfortunately, not become the equivalent of the male Mr.

As I didn't want my identity to be solely determined by my marital status, part of my motivation to complete the doctoral degree was the added incentive of escaping classification as either a Miss or a Mrs. Once I had my doctorate, I had a legitimate title—

Dr.—regardless of my marital status. However, I later faced another dilemma. My husband wanted me to change my name.

My husband was brought up to value himself, to be proud of himself and his heritage. His family is respected in the community and he is, justifiably, proud of his origins, proud of his family ties, and proud of his name. Until he fell in love with me, he fully expected that his future wife would want to assume his name, become identified with himself and his family. They would be Mr. and Mrs. T.

When we decided to get married, he was hurt that I had no desire to give up my name, my identity. While he understood that I was invested in keeping my name for professional reasons, he wanted me to adopt his name. We spent many hours discussing this issue. I patiently explained my perspective, going into detail about the symbolic meaning of changing my name—that it would mean giving up my identity, exchanging it for his, becoming subservient to him. I even proposed a compromise, that we might both change our names to one that would incorporate each of our identities.

My husband is a warm, kind, considerate, caring human being. He isn't insensitive. I wouldn't have married him if he were. Yet he genuinely couldn't understand why I didn't want his name. If I was proud to become his wife, why wouldn't I want to acknowledge this publicly by adopting his name? Even though he continued to have difficulty with my stubborn refusal to change my name, he swallowed his pride and married me anyway.

My name continues to be a sore spot with my husband. Every now and again the issue resurfaces in one form or another. As much as he loves me, he wishes I could be more traditional, more like "regular people." And, in his circles, I am unusual, for most of his relatives, and purportedly all of his business associates, are married to their Mrs.

Whenever we talk about my name we have a similar discussion, then retreat back to our respective positions. While we understand each other, we wish it could be different. He wishes I were more of a conventional wife, and I yearn for his support of my feminist stance.

As most women change their names when they get married, many people assume that I am Mrs. T. When dealing with people such as school personnel and service technicians, it doesn't serve any purpose to correct whoever has made this assumption. However, I am often confused about what to do with people who have known me for many years and "should" know my name.

Some people continue to send mail, ostensibly intended for me, but addressed to a Mrs. W. T. When I was once recovering from surgery, someone sent a get-well card to the hospital. Months later, it was returned to them. There was no Mrs. W. T. in the hospital.

Adding a Mrs. in front of my husband's name doesn't make it mine. My name is Lesley. It wouldn't begin with a W., even if I had followed social convention and elected to change my last name. Mrs. W. T. is expendable, easily replaceable. Anyone can become her. All they have to do is change their name. And I, Lesley Irene Shore, am not an expendable item.

Even with my insights and convictions, it has been difficult holding onto my name. I could easily have avoided the internal conflict, pleased my husband, and escaped dealing with the confusions and explanations that keeping my name has necessitated. This one small stand has been complicated and problematic. I do it because of the larger issue.

The matter of my name, my title, isn't nearly as important as the underlying issue—entitlement. Despite all the gains we have made with women's liberation, women continue to be subtly disempowered. And we inadvertently collude with society in this process. Changing our names is symptomatic of our lack of entitlement.

It is well known that women tend to have difficulty asserting themselves; we don't feel entitled. A number of years ago assertiveness training courses proliferated the mental health field. Women flocked to take these classes which promised to teach us how to stand up to others, hold our ground, stick up for ourselves. But while many women learned a great deal in these classes, they had difficulty using the skills in their lives. They readily reverted to old patterns, for the underlying issue hadn't been addressed.

A precursor of assertiveness is entitlement. Once a woman feels entitled to something, then and only then is she able to work toward obtaining it for herself. And she usually doesn't need to learn assertiveness skills once she feels entitled. When someone feels entitled to something, this expectation communicates itself adequately enough.

Much of my work with women, especially during the early phases of therapy, centers around entitlement. Most women are overly attuned to taking care of other people. They are inclined to empathize with others and attend to their needs, often at the expense of their own. I, therefore, frequently invite women to begin giving themselves the same consideration they give to other people, and encourage them to see themselves as entitled to wishes and desires of their own—to be advocates for themselves as well as others. Women often have difficulty with this concept, proclaiming that such behavior on their part would be selfish. Advocating for their selves is self-ish, ringing of too much self-interest, self-involvement.

Some of my colleagues use the phrase "giving one-self permission" rather than "entitlement," and I considered using this phrase with clients. However, *we do not need permission for something we are entitled to have*. In my mind, the issue is more basic. It is an inherent right, something given, something that comes with the territory.

Wanting to further clarify the notion of entitlement, I resorted to looking it up in the dictionary. I was trying to discover why the word has such a loaded meaning. According to *Webster's New Collegiate Dictionary* (1974), "entitle" refers to having the proper grounds for seeking or claiming something. The example given was "this ticket" entitles "the bearer to free admission."

Unfortunately, a woman doesn't bear the ticket for admission. We aren't supposed to embody the masculine and can't "stick up" for ourselves. What comes with the territory of being a woman, is lack of entitlement, lack of having the proper grounds for seeking something for ourselves.

A "feminine" woman is supposed to be self-denying and self-sacrificing. While we have supposedly graduated from being servants, we are still expected to serve others, to minister to their needs. Moreover, we are to do so without considering ourselves, without having a thought or a feeling about its affect on us. Other people come first.

Society expects a woman to serve the needs of others, not of her self. We're not allowed to have a self. A self would have an identity, a name. We're to be self-less, not self-ish.

A woman's selfhood depends upon her ability to captivate and capture a man. We learn this lesson early, for we are fed the fairy tale that finding Prince Charming, changing our name, and riding off into the sunset with him will lead to living happily ever after. Only then will we have a name we can keep. Already as little girls, we want to become Mrs. We aren't entitled.

It wasn't so long ago that women were unable to vote. We weren't entitled to a voice in who runs this country, what laws it has, or who decides the laws. While we have won the right to vote, society continues limiting our power by undermining our sense of our selves.

It is impossible for women to grow up feeling entitled in a world dominated by the masculine. We don't have the ticket for full-fledged admission. We don't possess a title—our own name.

Belly Breathing

In my college days we weren't supposed to notice that the professors were primarily men. We weren't supposed to notice that the books were written by people with male names. We weren't supposed to notice that the names we memorized to match the theories were mainly male. And I didn't notice. At least I didn't until I wanted to enter "society."

When the time came to graduate from college, I went to the placement office to begin finding a job. It was more than an enlightening experience. It was a rude awakening.

First I explained my situation. I told them that I had majored in psychology and hoped to find related employment. They looked at me kindly, then asked a deadly question. "Can you type?" Although somewhat confused about what this had to do with finding a job, I answered: "Yes, in a fashion, at least well enough to type my term papers," though I couldn't attest to the exact number of words per minute. Reassured by my response, the placement officer promised that if I could type, they could certainly find me a job as a secretary.

Although perturbed and upset, I didn't inquire whether they asked male graduates similar questions. They obviously didn't. Looking back on these events, I don't recall feeling outraged by the obvious sexism. I was too worried about my future. What would I do

next? I didn't think to persist, or argue, or fight. I un-
questioningly accepted all that came along with my
female inheritance.

After years of living in a world dominated by the
masculine, an important part of myself had been closed
off from experience, banished from awareness, lost. I
wasn't connected with the part that felt an injustice
had been done. And while I recognized that I was cut off
from "society," I didn't realize I'd incorporated this attitude inside myself. I was cut off from my self and didn't
understand the restlessness beneath my surface, my
sense of incompleteness, and continual searching.

Much later in life, my search for "something"
brought me to a yoga class. Taking a colleague's suggestion I went to one class, only to be initially disap-
pointed. I had expected to push my body to do complicated, strenuous tasks. Instead, the teacher slowly led
us through a series of moves designed to stretch muscles as well as strengthen them. She focused primarily
on the back, an area I didn't even look at in the mirror.
Between each move she instructed us to relax—to lie
there and breathe slow, deep, rhythmic breaths. It felt
too slow for me. How could I accomplish anything if I
was "just" lying there breathing? Rather than appreciate this rare opportunity to breathe, I thought about
the time I was wasting.

Yet, "something" compelled me to continue my
yoga lessons.

The first lesson seemed simple. I merely needed to
breathe properly. Yoga breathing is breathing from the
belly, taking long, deep, slow, complete breaths. In order to do this I had to pay attention to my breath, not
take it for granted. And once I began focusing on my

breath, I was surprised to discover that I wasn't taking complete breaths. I was holding my stomach in, making sure my belly didn't protrude.

When I was younger, women wore girdles. Even though I no longer wore a girdle, I was holding my stomach in. I'd learned how to constrict my stomach muscles, suck in my stomach, and had never noticed this made it impossible to breathe a complete breath. All those years of holding my stomach in—and never sensing that I wasn't breathing properly.

My yoga teacher talked with us about belly breathing. She told us that babies take complete breaths. They breathe with their bellies, not just the top part of their lungs. She pointed out that if we watch infants breathing, we can easily see their bellies moving in and out with each breath. Their stomachs expand as they breathe in, and contract as they breathe out. Listening to her, I realized that I too must have known how to breathe properly. Somewhere along the line I lost touch with those inner messages.

While I don't know when I stopped breathing the natural way, I do know that I became concerned about my appearance, and began holding my stomach in. Rather than expose my stomach, I pulled it inside my body, and hid it there. As my belly was occupying too much space, there was not much room for air. Refusing to pay attention to these internal cues, I forced my body to breathe unnatural, short, constricted breaths, and I no longer knew how to take a complete breath.

It was difficult unlearning all those years of training—many years of holding onto my stomach and constricting my breath. I had to stop worrying about my bulging belly, release my stomach muscles, and allow my belly to expand and contract. I had to let my body do what it already knew how to do—breathe.

At first this required thought. I had to make sure I was taking a breath that fully expanded my lungs. It took quite a while before I was able to breathe properly without thinking about it, without consciously attending to it. During this process the breath taught me other important lessons.

The breath is one of the few involuntary bodily activities readily affected by thought. We can consciously breathe in a deep breath, hold our breath, and exhale over an extended period of time. We can slow down our breath or speed it up, all under conscious control. Yet the cycle of breathing continues, whether or not we attend to it, whether or not we are conscious of it.

When we're not thinking about the breath, our autonomic nervous system takes over. We breathe steadily, one breath rhythmically following another. During sleep our breath slows its pace, becomes shallow. While exercising our breath speeds up, keeping pace with our body's requirements for fresh breath.

Whenever our bodies aren't getting enough oxygen, they automatically attempt to breathe in more air. Usually these adjustments deal with the problem. But if we are still unable to get enough oxygen into our bodies, we need to become aware that a problem exists. Anxiety is nature's way of alerting us to a potential danger, warning us that something bad is about to happen.

There are many reasons why women are prone to anxiety. One generally overlooked reason has to do with the attitude towards women's stomachs. Most women learn to tighten their stomach muscles, suck in their stomachs, stuff their bellies inside their bodies, and hide them there. We are, consequently, unable to breathe properly. Women are prone to having anxiety attacks because our bodies are trying to tell us that we're not getting enough oxygen.

Even though most women have rounded bellies, we're taught that, in order to look attractive, we should have flat stomachs. Attempting to accomplish the impossible, to make that belly disappear, we struggle to hold our stomachs in, suck in our guts. We walk around practically holding our breath for fear that our stomachs might protrude. And as we can't take complete breaths, we take mini breaths—short little gaspy breaths that don't get enough oxygen into our systems.

When the brain senses that we need more oxygen it begins sending messages to the body—requests for more oxygen, demands for more breath. The body revs up its breathing. As it can't take a whole breath, it takes lots and lots of mini breaths. When these don't add up to a complete breath the body again cries out for more oxygen, sends increasingly insistent messages to the brain. Again the brain tries. It transmits messages to all the right places, but all they can do is breathe faster and faster, take more and more mini breaths, little gasps of air, over and over and over.

I have just described an anxiety attack. It is pure panic—a frightening experience. It can happen "merely" because women have lost the ability to take a complete breath—a breath that fills the belly, the lungs, the entire chest cavity with oxygen. We're trained to disregard our body's signals, to hold our stomachs in, constrict our breath.

My yoga experience helped me recognize that I was dissociated from my body, particularly my belly. I'd separated myself from this part of my body, no longer listened to its signals, and didn't know I wasn't breathing properly. I was cut off from parts of myself that were being abused. I "didn't notice."

Abuse

Many of my clients have been abused. In my early years as a therapist it took a while before they felt comfortable enough in our relationship to talk about the abuse. They were ashamed of what had happened and had often never confided in anyone.

As I grew in experience, I found myself asking certain clients whether they had been abused. While this wasn't a question I usually asked during a first session, I sometimes found myself asking it then. I was amazed that those I asked said they had been abused, and either proceeded to tell me about it, or indicated they weren't ready to talk. In retrospect, I had sensed the signs before I could articulate them. I was recognizing the symptoms of abuse.

In more recent years, we have become increasingly adept at identifying symptoms associated with earlier abuse. It is now generally recognized that many people who describe experiences of being outside their bodies, sometimes looking down and watching, other times leaving and going somewhere else, have experienced some form of abuse. They learned to separate from their bodies as a way of surviving the abuse, as a means of living through it. They dissociate.

Dissociation is a defense mechanism. It refers to the process whereby a group of psychological activities, possessing a certain unity among themselves, separate from the rest of the personality. Freud originally wrote about dissociated states when he investigated the symptoms of his hysterical patients—people with physical symptoms, such as a paralyzed hand, for which there was no physical cause. While he brilliantly recognized that these symptoms were expressions of some dissociated aspect of the self, he refused to believe his patients' descriptions of sexual abuse. He attributed their accounts to fantasy—as having arisen out of a wish. I suspect his patients were abused.

The process of dissociation is most clearly apparent in people with a multiple personality. In multiple personalities the dissociations are complete, resulting in separate personalities. Different people co-exist in the same body. These "people" can be of either sex, for there are often both male and female subpersonalities.

We know that multiple personalities arise from severe physical abuse, often sexual. Sybil, a popularized account of one such multiple personality, was characteristically found to have been severely abused as a child. Dissociation is a coping mechanism. The person endures the abuse by not being fully there, by separating off the part of the self that has to be there, while the rest goes someplace else.

Whenever I have a client who reports dissociative experiences, experiences where they separate from their bodies, I now look for a history of abuse. Sometimes the dissociation isn't obvious, but is described more as feeling "different," being "out of it," not feeling completely themselves, "weird." These experiences are not limited to women, for a few of my male clients have described similar sensations. They too were abused.

Once I was more adept at identifying dissociated

states, particularly after becoming familiar with the dissociated state of hypnosis, I realized that there are many occasions when people describe experiences of not being fully present in their bodies. They speak of feeling as if "something else takes over," not being themselves at the time, it "just happens." When I ask for more details, they have trouble giving me any. These descriptions are especially typical of the way women describe their symptoms of bulimia and compulsive eating. I began suspecting that they were describing dissociated states.

Listening closely to women describing their eating patterns, I heard dissociated themes: The hand begins reaching for the cookie jar. It seems to have its own mind, for it moves on its own volition—reaching into the jar, grabbing food, and rapidly shoving it into the mouth. There is no thought, no awareness, only speed and a compelling intensity that takes over, possesses them. Sometimes the body frantically runs to the store and grabs more food, so that the hand can continue pushing food into the mouth. They're driven to do this until . . . .

Later, when awareness returns, they feel shame. Deeply ashamed of their behavior, they vow to undo the damage that was done. Compulsive eaters promise to diet the very next day. Bulimics immediately purge themselves of food they so rapidly consumed, being driven to do so, for they are not yet aware of what's happening. They have to do it. It's as if they are in a trance, a dissociated state.

After hearing similar descriptions from many women, I began wondering why they were describing dissociated states. I suspected they might have been abused. When I inquired about possible abuse, I learned that only some had been abused. Most of them described "normal" developmental experiences.

As more and more women shared their difficulties with me, I heard the same theme over and over again. Compulsive eaters kept describing "something" taking over. Bulimics were similarly articulating the cycle of binging and purging. More and more women were talking about being out of touch with themselves, not being fully present in their bodies. More and more women were complaining of uncontrollable urges that drove them to eat. I kept wondering what was going on. And how could a compulsive eater's experience be similar to that of women who had been abused? What could be the connection?

Then it hit me! There must be something about the way women develop. Something inherent in their experience which predisposes them to these dissociative states. But what could that be? Then it really hit me. Abuse! All women experience some form of abuse. Abuse is inherent in the experience of growing up as a female in this society. The feminine is abused.

I began thinking about my female clients and recalled the "minor" abuses that were part of their development. Practically all of them had related at least one incident when they were sexually approached, usually during adolescence, by a member of the opposite sex. Sometimes it had been a boy their own age, more often an adult—from a building contractor working on the family home to the parent of a best friend. Many had allowed themselves to be touched or otherwise manhandled. They did not welcome the experience, but somehow endured it. Each of them hesitated to talk about the events and felt ashamed of what had happened—as if they had done something wrong. Even when "nothing happened," when they were able to prevent further advances, they never told anyone, not even a parent. I was generally the first person they had been able to tell.

While the issue of abuse has finally been granted some credibility, it is still a vastly unexplored area. Only glaring abuse is acknowledged. And when it comes to sexual abuse, the notion of whether or not "she asked for it" still raises its specter. Yet, as I delved deeper into this issue, I realized that every woman experiences abuse.

Looking back over my own past, I remembered many times when I was subjected to unwanted sexual advances. It was always difficult dealing with leers, snickers and whistles of passers-by. While they felt like invasions, they were delivered as if offering a compliment. There were unwelcome pinches on my rear end, and times when a man's body rubbed against mine while trapped in a crowded subway car. Dating was always fraught with the dilemma of how to deal with unwanted sexual advances, especially during those adolescent years when I desperately wanted boys to like me.

My female clients describe similar experiences. Some were severely damaged by instances of abuse. One such client, a well endowed young woman, felt ashamed and embarrassed about her breasts. She kept herself overweight and wore baggy clothing in an attempt to keep men from making sexual remarks. These attempts were to no avail. She was frequently the recipient of whistles and sexual comments whenever she walked near a man. It came to the point where she was afraid to leave her apartment and go to a store by herself. Petrified that something might happen to her, that a man might make a pass at her or otherwise assault her sexually, she stayed inside and pulled down the shades.

I had never considered the issue of obscene phone calls until I attended a psychological conference on women. One of the presenters asked for a show of hands from the audience, primarily women, of those who had received an obscene phone call. From where I was sitting, every woman raised her hand. I know that I lost count of how many such calls I have received. And I had never previously thought of these phone calls as abusive, merely annoyances. But they are.

Once my eyes opened, I started seeing the pervasiveness of abusive behavior towards women. Everywhere I looked I could see abuse. It isn't always sexual, and sometimes it's subtle. But abuse is abuse. And it's apparently taken for granted, never questioned, inherent in the condition of being female.

The more I became convinced of the ubiquitousness of abusive behavior towards women, the more confused I became. The men I know aren't evil. And yet men abuse women. The more I thought about this issue, the more I suspected an underlying process. It began making sense when I recognized abuse as a symptom of a deeper dynamic, something unconsciously enacted between masculine and feminine.

When men suppress the feminine aspects of their selves, they become unbalanced, over-masculinized, macho. They don't have the softness and caring of the feminine to balance their aggression. Men are, thereby, prone to re-enact the supremacy of the masculine with women who inadvertently play the part of the victimized feminine.

I suspect that when men abuse women they are persecuting the feminine displaced outside their selves. They have unconsciously become prisoners of their own masculine maintaining suppression of their feminine. Their internal dynamics between masculine and feminine are externalized—enacted between male and female. And in this way men and women are condemned to compulsively repeat society's imbalances. We unconsciously act them out with each other.

Men not only seem to expect women to welcome their attention, but they also appear to feel entitled to patronize and otherwise humiliate us. They take advantage of woman's position, lauding their power over us, subtly reminding us that "she" is "his" victim. It's as if they take every occasion to reinforce their position, their status as males, of woman's position in relation to man, of masculine to feminine. This attitude is often disguised in behavior that may appear innocuous, but is intrusive.

Recently, a singing gorilla interrupted my hair cut to deliver balloons in celebration of the hair stylist's birthday. After singing his birthday song he put his arm around the very attractive stylist, handed her the balloons, and demanded a few kisses. Not to be a party pooper she gave him one, but, from my vantage point, was not eager to do so. She obviously cringed as her lips touched his hairy head. She wasn't inclined to kiss strangers, even a stranger bearing gifts, masquerading in a gorilla's costume.

There are countless instances of subtle abuse.

Some occur when men treat women in a subservient
manner. Women are expected to serve and are often
ministering to the needs of others. This expectation,
depending on the context, can be demeaning and could
be considered a subtle form of abuse. While women are
sometimes paid for this work, we are often merely expected to do it. Even when paid, we can still be subjected to additional abuse. For example, I've often
watched waitresses shrink back in response to a male
customer putting his arm around her and calling her
"dear." Her wishes are irrelevant. She doesn't necessarily want him to touch her or feel endearing towards
him, but she puts up with this behavior for fear of
insulting a customer who is only being "friendly." She
is expected to tolerate the unwelcome physical contact.

These are a few of the many "minor" abuses which
are considered acceptable in this society, expressions
of man's "interest," prurient though it may be. These
experiences are rarely discussed, shared or acknowledged, for females are given the message that we
should be flattered to be the objects of male attention. I
began hearing a different story once I let my clients
know that I understood, that I was interested, that I
cared about their real feelings and valued their experience. Only then could they share their rage, their out-
rage, their feelings of having been invaded, violated,
raped.

Females grow up in one large extended dysfunctional family—society. My clients taught me about the
abuse, and what happens to us afterwards. While we
initially recognize that we've been abused, we are
given the hidden, or not so hidden, message that we
shouldn't feel this way. Sometimes we're ridiculed for

reacting with displeasure to a "minor" abuse. And although we may know what it is we feel, we grow to distrust our feelings when they are invalidated by others, by men, by society. We then split this feeling off, hide it from ourselves, talk ourselves into not feeling the feeling. We separate a part of our selves off from ourselves. We dissociate.

Abuse comes with the territory of being a woman.

Up Rooted

Most women direct their energy outside, focusing on other people. In my experience, very few women are also grounded in themselves. An essential aspect is cut off at the center of our being, in our femaleness. We are unable to become rooted in the soil of our selves, for this central place is dissociated, dispossessed, disowned. As we're cut off from our center, from the feminine, our development is short-circuited—shunted away from the earth within. We aim to please and become overly invested outside, in other people.

One of my clients typifies this stance. "Doris" is a very bright, capable, educated woman with business as well as domestic skills. Yet she evaluates herself as worthless and devotes herself to meeting the needs of others. Most of her energy is directed towards making other people happy.

In one particular session Doris poignantly described a dinner out with her husband. While he has many opportunities to frequent good restaurants as part of his job, it's a special event for her. More typically, she does the cooking and is reputed to be an excellent cook. She appreciates good food and looks forward to those rare occasions when she and her husband go to a nice restaurant for a quiet dinner together, just the two of them.

Doris had made many gains in therapy. When she

first came to see me she was very depressed. She was unable to recognize her wants and generally felt undeserving. After much hard work, she was beginning to identify a few things she wanted for herself. And while she was still having trouble feeling entitled to wanting these things, she did want to go out for dinner with her husband.

They went to a nice restaurant. As they studied the menu Doris was well aware of her husband's usual inclination towards eating meat. Yet he asked her about the lobster, inquired about the sauce, and wondered if he might like it. She described it to him, knowing that she was also interested in that selection.

When her husband decided to order lobster, Doris was faced with a dilemma, a dilemma for which she saw only one solution. While he had freely chosen to order lobster, she was afraid he would not enjoy it. Knowing his usual preference for meat, she felt she had to order it for herself, even though there were other dishes more to her liking. Her primary consideration was ensuring that he enjoy his meal, and if the one he ordered was not to his liking, she felt she had to be able to offer him one that would please. Just to be safe, she ordered the beef.

Their meals arrived and her husband was delighted with his lobster. When he offered her some she was unable to take any. Even though she wanted a taste, she could not bear to deprive him of even a morsel of pleasure. He tried to insist, but she could not allow herself to have any. Her husband had no difficulty availing himself of the meat on her plate. Still, she could not take from his.

Doris' connection and caring for others isn't bal-

anced by an investment in herself. She isn't grounded
inside her self. And while she struggles to feel good-
enough, she never manages to nullify her inherent
sense of worthlessness, her badness, by pleasing other
people.

Many women are overly attuned to picking up
cues from others, finding ways of meeting their needs,
sensing what another person wants. It's as if we have
antennas constantly moving around, finding the best
position to pick up waves emanating from other people.
These antennas have been around a long time. Often
they begin to grow during childhood, finding ways of
pleasing a parent, a friend, a peer group, a teacher.

Women refine the art of tuning into other people
by disregarding internal cues, our inner voice. This
inner voice may be crying out, calling to us, waiting to
be heard. It knows about inside, about unmet needs
and unanswered desires. But as our antennas are generally busy only focusing outward, we don't hear these
cries from within. We are up-rooted—unable to hear
our inner voices crying out to be heard.

Many women are also depressed. They describe
feeling empty and depleted. After caring for other people, always giving to them, they're running on empty.
All their reserves are used up, and nothing is left.
We're supreme nurturers—of other people.

Women are expected to be the source of endless
supplies. And as the female breast symbolizes nurturance, it isn't surprising that an abundant bosom is
valued by our society. This part of a woman is encouraged to be voluptuously round, for it's the part that
gives to other people.

Even though men appear to value large breasts, at

least judging by the pictures they apparently admire, women speak differently about their breasts. While women with small breasts may wish to appear more feminine, less flat-chested, even they prefer not to be encumbered by a large bosom. Large breasts are heavy and physically uncomfortable. It is difficult to move without feeling them bouncing around.

While there are physical reasons why women dislike having abundant bosoms, I've learned that we aren't necessarily talking about the physical aspects of our breasts. When we talk about our breasts we're often talking symbolically. We're talking about our capacity to give to others.

I've heard many women, even those with small breasts, put it quite bluntly, saying that they're tired of being seen as "one big tit." And while these women are primarily referring to their nurturing role, they are also talking about being seen as a sex object. Under both circumstances they feel expected to take care of someone else's needs, whether those needs be for succor or sex.

When women talk about being depleted, running on empty, they often go on to say that they've been "sucked dry." There is nothing left of them to give, for they've been "milked" to death. They are tired of giving to others and receiving little in return. These women are not talking about the condition of their breasts. They're describing their emptiness, their inner depletion. This sense of feeling drained is a feature of depression common among many women.

The association between a woman's breast and her capacity to nurture others can, at times, underlie other attitudes and behaviors. For example, one of my clients, "Claire," came in for a session announcing that she would be having breast reduction surgery. As we had never discussed the surgery, I was surprised by the apparent abruptness of her decision. And since I generally encourage clients to explore feelings rather than act them out, I suggested we discuss the surgery.

After some discussion, it appeared that Claire's surgery had a symbolic meaning. She was retreating from the position of being the supreme nurturer, the source of endless supplies. As she was feeling more entitled to her own needs, she was beginning to say "no" to other people. She was struggling to balance her caring for others by investing in her self, and her surgery was an important aspect of making this internal shift. Even though her husband was against the surgery, Claire believed she was having it purely for aesthetic and health reasons. As I suspected she was also trying to say that she no longer wished to be seen as having endless supplies, that she has her limits, I wondered whether she might find another way of communicating this information to her husband as well as other people.

Claire proceeded with the surgery and was pleased with the results. But she still needed to deal with her underlying issues, for the surgery hadn't addressed the deeper feelings she had about herself or helped her establish a positive relationship with her body. On the contrary, she had invited someone to cut into a feminine part of herself. In a later chapter, "Entitling," I'll describe the process by which Claire later worked through these issues. But until she was able to do so, she remained disconnected from her center and haunted by unresolved feelings.

All too many females are cut off from their center, from the feminine, from their source. Looking to become rooted in the good, we send our roots outside ourselves and try to absorb goodness into our being so that we too may become good. We look for self acceptance and focus on externals, including our external selves—our bodies, our appearance. But we still feel "bad."

Ashamed

I used to confuse shame and guilt. Then I attended a lecture where the presenter differentiated between these two emotions. She described guilt as being associated with behavior, with an unacceptable action. We, therefore, feel guilty after we have done something that we shouldn't have done, or feel we shouldn't have done. In contrast, shame is associated with the self. It has to do with an aspect of the self that is unacceptable. While guilt has to do with behavior, shame is connected with the person.

Having benefited from this clarification, I began hearing differently. When clients talked about feeling guilty, they were often describing shame. Most of them were also depressed. They felt "bad."

My female clients often describe feeling worthless and useless. And while I was used to hearing them talk about feeling "bad," I had previously categorized these feelings as "depression." I was taught that depression is anger turned inward. Now I also hear shame.

When I began attending to shame, I noticed that clients often have difficulty exploring this feeling. Their sense of shame is generally unspoken, difficult to address. My questions tap an unexplored aspect.

"Doris," however, was articulate about her shame. During our first session she sat dejected, staring at the floor. Her potentially pretty face seemed flat and empty, and her muted, drab clothing matched her expression. It lacked luster. Her voice was a monotone, trailing off into nowhere. She appeared drained— drained of expression, drained of possibility.

When we spoke of her reasons for coming to see me, she could barely express her despair and hopelessness. She appeared resigned to her condition—as if she had lost whatever hope had ever been present. Describing herself as not being worth anything, not being worth having friends or people to love her, she clearly felt badly about her self. She devotes herself to her husband and family, hoping to be valued by them and, thereby, feel better about herself. Instead, she feels taken for granted at best, and more generally put down, demeaned, "walked on" by everyone in her family. Stating that she may be lying down on the floor, allowing others to walk all over her, was even said with a note of self-criticism—further proof of her inadequacy.

As we probed further, Doris spoke of her deep-seated sense of shame. While she could almost hear her mother's voice saying "You should be ashamed of yourself," her shame wasn't connected to any specific action or behavior. It was intrinsic to existence, rooted in her self, permeating every aspect of her being. She felt ashamed, worthless.

While many women don't directly address their shame, they often talk about feeling ashamed of their bodies. Their sense of shame is displaced onto the body.

All my female clients express displeasure with their bodies. While more slender women talk about being too skinny, not having a feminine appearance, rounder clients complain about being too heavy, fat. Some criticize their breasts. Others condemn their thighs, hips, or waist. Many complain about their stomachs. No matter which part is the object of derision, they describe that part with disgust.

Women are ashamed of their bodies. Many wish to cover up, hide. My heavier clients are ashamed to be seen in bathing suits. As they can't bear exposing themselves to others, they deprive themselves of potential pleasure at the beach. Thinner clients complain about their bones showing.

Ashamed to be seen as we really are, we resort to camouflaging ourselves. We disguise ourselves in costumes and social masks aimed to make us appear less flawed, more acceptable. The clothing and cosmetic industries aid and abet this process by subtly insinuating that we must hide our real selves. Faces are hidden behind masks of make-up, with some women unable to appear in public without their "faces on." Multimillion dollar industries thrive on women's sense of shame.

Plastic surgery takes advantage of women's shame by encouraging us to consider changing our features. Under the guise of offering women options, the medical community persuades women to allow them to attack our bodies. Many women succumb to surgery's seductive promise that we will become happy with our bodies, pleased with our selves.

Cosmetic surgery doesn't solve underlying psychological issues. "Helen" came to me long after breast augmentation surgery. After mentioning the surgery, she went on to tell me that she now despises her stomach. Her negative feelings had moved from her breasts to her stomach. To her credit, Helen recognized that she displaces other feelings onto her body. Someone else might have subjected her body to another surgical procedure, only to discover another part, then another, and another as the focus of her negative feelings, her shame.

I began wondering why women make so many disparaging remarks about their bodies. Why are we ashamed of our bodies? After mulling these questions over for quite some time, I realized that it made perfect sense. Not only does society value appearances, externals, but a woman's body is a reminder of her second-class citizenship. Her body embodies the feminine, her female self, the "bad" part of her self.

Once I translated "body" to mean "female self," I was astounded to realize that a woman's innermost sense of herself, her inner nature, is associated with shame. This shouldn't have come as a surprise considering our society's orientation towards the feminine. But it did. I then recognized that society's devaluation and suppression of the feminine contributes to woman's underlying sense of shame. Women can never be good enough because we are identified with the feminine.

Even though we attempt to separate, dissociate, from our badness, we cannot totally escape from ourselves. Our shame is a reminder. It reminds us that a part has been disowned, a part that is bad or unacceptable.

A woman's shame is a vestige, a left-over remnant from her dissociated part. It reminds her of her badness. This sense of being bad is often displaced onto her body. As she then struggles with her body, trying to make it good, she ends up re-enacting the original dissociation. She cannot be fully present in her body; she separates from it, dissociates. But she cannot escape her shame. It follows her everywhere she goes, wherever she is. She is ashamed.

In Her Moon

My memories of childhood are hazy—fleeting pictures interspersed with vague scenarios. I have clearer recollections of adolescence, though they too are shrouded in mist. There were clouds hovering over my development, casting shadows on my life. It has taken me many years to learn about these clouds, allow them to shed their tears, clear the air. Looking back over my past, I see shadows—the shadows of war.

I used to blame the Second World War for all my troubles, my sadness, my strife. There are still times, always during the dark of night, when airplanes flying overhead occasion moments of panic and thoughts of imminent danger. While I worry about an enemy attack, I now know that these fears are vestigial, remnants of earlier memories. Even though I have no clear memory of air raids, the sounds of bombers or the havoc they wrecked, I was apparently affected by the experience.

The Second World War was an obvious war—a war we can name, define, talk about, eventually move through and put behind us. Its content is manifest, with battles fought on the surface, available to be seen. Undeclared wars are more difficult to deal with. They are surreptitious wars, concealed and covert. Their battles are hidden, their hostility unacknowledged. We can't talk about these wars.

Society's campaign against the feminine is one such undeclared war. It is a war waged on many fronts, and a major battle in this undeclared war is waged inside women.

While the covert war against the feminine is present from the moment of birth, affecting all stages of female development, it escalates during puberty when a girl's body becomes more characteristically female and her identity is solidifying. This battle becomes part of herself. It also contributes to the development of eating disorders, depression, and other dysfunctional symptoms.

My own adolescence was touched by this war. There were early warnings, signs, portents of danger lurking ahead. When I developed cravings, I had no sense of their origins, their roots inside myself. I knew I wanted "something," and was inclined to focus outside myself, look for "it" there. I attached my cravings onto potato chips, Twinkies and other sources of external nurturance.

Even though I had previously been slender, my cravings began taking their toll. Kindly adults started hinting about my weight, suggesting I watch my food intake. But my cravings persisted, unabated. They were getting worse, rather than better. And those who watched my body changing shape kept raising their voices in warning. They began confronting me, telling me I needed to take control, force my self to refrain from eating, begin to diet. I was expected to battle with my body.

Eventually I submitted to the voices and started the first of many diets. The diet was "successful," for I had large reserves of will power, and readily returned to my more slender shape. I "won" this first battle.

During adolescence a girl's body becomes that of a woman, capable of symbolically representing her full-fledged femaleness. The power of the feminine is developing. She becomes a threat.

When a girl enters puberty she experiences stirrings of her natural femaleness. Her whole body changes shape, and her breasts develop. She grows body hair. Then she gets her period. All these changes are met with ambivalence. She is placed in a double bind—wishing to embrace these changes in her body, yet compelled to reject them.

On one hand, these changes are experienced with joy, for they indicate that she is growing, developing signs that identify her with her mother. She is thrilled to be growing up, becoming a woman. However, these changes have subtle negative connotations, for it is not inherently wonderful to be a woman in this culture—a culture that is at war with the feminine now stirring within her.

How is this pubescent girl to deal with these mixed feelings? As it's a covert war, she doesn't recognize the battle taking shape. She can't talk about it, for she doesn't have the words. All too often her mother can't help. She, too, is immersed in the battle.

The onset of adolescence initiates a girl's life-long battle with her body—its natural shape, cycle, hairiness and aroma. Any evidence of the feminine within is suspect, cause for alarm. She must be ever on guard, prepared for battle, ready to attack. Society induces her to try holding onto her prepubescent body in efforts to ward off the feminine.

Much against her body's requirements for adequate nutrition, she is encouraged to diet to maintain her lack of hips, buttocks and stomach. When her body naturally rebels with hunger, she has urges to eat. These bodily urges, potential manifestations of the feminine within, can't be trusted. She must fight them, overcome them. Rather than hear these urges as her body's plea for healthy nutrients, she tries to suppress them, push them away. But sometimes she can't. The urges feel too strong. They overpower her, and she is compelled to eat. This is a battle she can't win. No matter what happens, she loses.

Some girls become preoccupied with this battle. Their fears of getting fat, gaining weight, grow into an obsession. They are ever on guard against the enemy, waging war on any sign of rounding stomach or softening surface. Every bite of food, any fraction of a calorie, is counted as a battle casualty. They battle so successfully that they prevent their bodies from developing, even stop their menses from arriving. Our society labels these girls as having a psychological problem, anorexia nervosa. We fail to acknowledge that they are fighting our wars for us, waging their private battle against the feminine. And while most girls don't go to this extreme, many fight a similar battle.

Despite attempts to diet, watch her weight, a girl's body usually develops curves, softness, fat. Many girls continue to battle against these signs going from one diet to another, trying to curtail their weight, contain their developing curvy shape. After a while their bodies become malnourished and their urges to eat become more compelling, overwhelming. They begin to binge. And as they cannot allow this lapse in their defenses to show, each binge necessitates that stricter measures be taken.

The battle is reinstated with a vengeance. Girls struggle to purge themselves of food, through vomiting, laxatives, exercise, or stricter dietary controls. Often binges are followed by fasting, which aggravates the body's already malnourished condition. The battle escalates, eventually becoming the well documented binge-purge (or diet) cycle characteristic of many eating disorders. This cycle is accompanied by shame.

Many girls talk about being ashamed of the amount of food they eat, wishing they had better control over their appetites, their cravings. They see the issue as a battle, a control battle. While they recognize that they are battling the curves and bulges, they are unable to address the larger war they are fighting— the battle against the feminine.

There are other enemies in this war against the feminine. Another enemy is hair. Prepubescent girls lack pubic hair, as well as hair under their arms and on their legs. This hairless body remains the "ideal," for it's an image untainted by signs of sexual maturity. Moreover, it simultaneously also differentiates her from the supposedly hairy, masculine body.

When the pubescent girl develops hair she is, again, placed in a double bind. She's proud of these signs of her physical maturity, yet condemned to battle with them, erase them from sight. And while she may gleefully yield a razor to her legs and under her arms in celebration of sexual maturity, she is, by this very act, eradicating all traces of developing sexuality. Razors, depilatories, and electrolysis are implements of destruction in the war against the feminine. She uses their power against her offensive hairs, trying to route out any sign of a feminine force lurking beneath the surface of her skin.

Menstruation is fraught with a similar double bind. While the onset of the menarche is an important development in a girl's life, there are no social rituals to celebrate, create a rite of passage. It is often kept hidden—surrounded by whispers and concealed items of clothing.

My therapy group for women discussed how they learned about their periods. All too often their mothers were too embarrassed to help them understand, let alone welcome, this event. Some were given a book and told to come to their mothers with any further questions. My clients immediately understood that these things couldn't be readily discussed. It was as if they had been handed a dirty book, filled with unspeakable and offensive information.

Some of my client's mothers were able to talk about menstruation. While these mothers were able to share the facts and explain the process, their communications were often tinged with subtle messages of shame. My clients took these messages as proof that something is wrong, bad. They reported feeling, deep down within themselves, in the core of their being, that something is wrong with them. The badness is inside. It has to do with their feminine flow. This is the enemy, the enemy within.

A woman's flow fully embodies the feminine. It comes from her center and is a primary target in the battle against the feminine. Even though men have hair under their arms and around their genitals, they never bleed from wombs. War is waged in earnest in this battle zone, with heavy artillery brought in to defeat the power of menstrual blood.

I have no clear memory of the day my menstrual blood started to flow. Instead, I have a vague sense of having been pleased and proud, and this pleasure seems surrounded by shame. In looking back on my adolescence, I recall a rather insignificant event that occurred some time later. While it wasn't a major event in my life, its images remain clear and vivid.

This memory is of a specific occasion when I had my period. I was very uncomfortable, for my periods were always painful—attended by severe cramps and general malaise. And though I felt dreadful, the only justifiable excuse for remaining home in bed was severe illness. So, cramps or no cramps, I went to school.

As the day progressed so did my lethargy and pain. I felt worse and worse. My energy was drained, the cramps unbearable. Nevertheless, I continued with my classes.

When I arrived at an afternoon class one of my fellow students, a male, approached me. We weren't close friends, or intimate in any way, but were friendly toward one another. He looked directly into my eyes and, with a voice that expressed genuine concern and caring, began inquiring into my health, asking me if I was feeling all right. I immediately averted my eyes, stammered that I felt "just fine," and rapidly took my seat.

After this brief conversation my attention was totally distracted from the content of the class. I was already preoccupied, dealing with pain, and was now also inundated by a myriad of conflicting feelings. While I hadn't wanted to lie to him, I was embarrassed to tell the truth. I couldn't tell him that I didn't feel fine at all, just had severe menstrual cramps. And, I hadn't really lied, for I was fine. Having my period was, supposedly, normal. Yet, I didn't feel this was normal. If "it" were normal, I would easily have told him about "it." I went around and around, obsessing about the situation, questioning myself, ruminating.

There was a part of me that felt ashamed. It was as if I were guarding a secret—something that was shameful, that he couldn't know about. And so I became absorbed with another worry. Did he know? How could he tell?

The class ended and again he approached me, inquiring into my health. He said that I appeared pale, that I looked unwell, and that he was worried about me. Perhaps I should go home, or at least see the school nurse. This time I tried to cover "it" up. I knew I couldn't tell him, confess. We just didn't talk about "those things." I put on my best smiling face, forced my voice to lilt, and cheerily thanked him for his concern. Then I proceeded to reassure him that I was "just fine" by accusing him of "imagining things." Walking down the corridor towards my next class, I felt alone, isolated from other people, accompanied only by pain.

In some ways I wasn't alone, for menstruating women have often been isolated, kept away from other people. Sometimes we've done this by choice—either wanting to be alone or seeking the company of other women at these times. More often it isn't by choice, for many traditions restrict and isolate women during their menstrual flow.

Our Judeo-Christian tradition judges menstruating women to be dirty, tainted, and unclean. Until relatively recently, they were forbidden to enter churches and synagogues. Orthodox Jewish tradition continues to ban menstruating women from their husbands beds. When their menses cease flowing their bodies are cleansed in a ritual bath. Only then are they permitted back. These customs condemn menstruating women, make them outcasts of their religion, their social world. They are contaminated, untouchable.

Even cultures which are respectful of the feminine, such as the Native American tradition, have taboos about a woman's monthly flow. Menstruating women are banned from attending their sacred sweat lodge ceremony. Medicine men are warned not to touch a woman who is in her cycle, for they could be negatively affected by her. A close friend of mine explained that Native Americans see women as being especially powerful during this time. Their taboos against a menstruating woman are borne out of respect for her power. It's believed that a medicine man can lose his power if he comes into contact with a woman who is "in her moon."

A woman's body cycles with the moon, keeps time with the moon. Her monthly cycle flows with the phases of the moon, for a cycle in the life of the moon around Earth corresponds to a cycle in the life of a woman on Earth. This connection between the moon and feminine flow is one of the great mysteries of nature. It is a mystery that has been long contemplated by humankind, and is as yet unsolved.

Another unsolved mystery has been observed in institutions and other situations where women live in close relationship with one another. Under these conditions their bodies begin cycling together, following the same rhythm, flowing in unison. The mystery of woman's blood is the mystery of the feminine, of nature, of creation.

The Greeks and Romans saw blood as the feminine essence that descends from the moon. The Bible views blood as the primary symbol of the life force, for ancient beliefs viewed people as having been literally made of their mothers' uterine blood, retained and coagulated into the form of a baby (Walker, 1983).

Women possess this mysterious power, the power of the feminine. Menstrual blood is a reminder of the feminine within, the dark side of the moon, the unseen, hidden, mysterious, and unknown. It is a woman's monthly reminder of her connection with the feminine, her participation in nature's cycles, creativity. As these red droplets carry such symbolic meaning, they have often been treated with wonder and respect. However, our society is a society ravaged by war, battling against the feminine, against nature. Menstruation is called "the curse."

A menstruating woman is a woman possessed—possessed by the feminine, the demon. She is under a spell, cursed. Her blood is offensive, repulsive, dirty, evil. In our war torn world she is evicted, thrown out, considered a traitor. Only when purified by bath or redeemed from having committed the sin of being female is she permitted to re-enter the social world.

While there are no formal initiation rites, a pubescent girl rapidly learns what is expected of her. She must cooperate in the war on the feminine by learning to control and camouflage any evidence of her female flow. It is no accident that television's menstruating maidens prance around in white bikinis, parading flat stomachs for the world to see. This image is in direct contrast to the realities of menstruation. Pubescent girls are indoctrinated in all the battle strategies necessary to imitate this fiction.

A pubescent girl is cajoled into purchasing the latest in "feminine protection," supporting a tampon industry which neglects to warn her that these items might be bleached, chemically treated to compress better, and possibly contain asbestos. Such warnings are irrelevant in a nation at war, a nation committed to stemming her flow, controlling "it." She is taught to put a plug inside herself. This keeps her from sensing her flow, disconnects her from the feminine within. Her blood is hidden, contained.

Even though a female may cooperate by plugging her flow, she soon learns not to wear white on "those days." Bleeding can become profuse, "accidents" happen, and clothing becomes stained. And while she may try to escape to the nearest bathroom, she can never be pure, purified of her stain, her tainted character.

A female body cycles. It changes, flowing from one phase to the next. And, as she moves into puberty, a girl begins identifying her cycle, recognizing its phases. However, she is not encouraged to become familiar with this cycle, to learn how to listen to her bodily signs, hear their messages and learn about herself. Instead, she is inducted into the war, instructed in its tactics, taught how to control and contain these phases. Her medicine chest becomes an armory, stocked with an armamentarium of pills and other battle supplies. In this war any evidence of her inner nature, whether secretion or smell, is cause for suspicion. Alarms are sounded. Battle ensues.

During the phase before her menses flow, a girl's

emotions tend to become more fluid. It's as if her insides are letting go, loosening up, starting to flow. She becomes emotionally labile. Her breasts may become sensitive and swell. Her stomach gets fuller, rounder, softer. While these changes may be normal for her, natural, she is taught that they are symptoms with a label, premenstrual syndrome. She is taught that she must manage this time by taking pills—pills to control her moods and pills to deal with her physical changes. She is taught the tactics of which pills to take when, swallowing their deadly poisons, incorporating them into her center, inviting them to battle with the feminine that is there.

When her blood starts to flow, she learns to take another pill. This one is for pain. It will help her deaden the messages from her body, enable her to force it to do things it may not wish to do. Given the help of these pills she can push herself to go to school, pretend she is "just fine."

Any irregularities in her cycle, though they may be normal for her, are treated. She's meted out pills to take on a daily basis, calculated to make her cycle "regular." It's of little concern that these pills may have other side effects, for they have been "proven" safe by the established medical battalion. If her juices flow mid-cycle, or if she ever develops a smell "there," she is admonished to wash herself with an assortment of chemicals, douche, and apply a feminine deodorant spray.

It's no wonder that the onset of menstruation brings with it mixed emotions for girls. While they may justifiably be pleased to be coming of age, they are now considered dirty and unclean. This notion has no basis in reality, for menstruation actually purifies a woman's body. Menstruation is nature's way of cleansing, moving out older, less viable, blood cells to make room for the new. It's nature's way of ensuring that a new life will have healthy, fertile soil to nurture its growth.

Our bodies are constantly eliminating waste products of natural functions. In addition to urinating and defecating, we blow our noses to discharge mucus, cough up phlegm from our lungs, expel carbon dioxide every time we breathe, perspire through pores, and shed tears of sadness from our eyes. While many of these natural functions are targets for social control, this is the only body function that is treated with such social revulsion, condemnation and shame.

Purchasing "sanitary" napkins and then disposing of them once they are no longer sanitary is often attended with feelings of shame, embarrassment. Many women report having mixed feelings when they approach the check-out counter with boxes of their "supplies" only to spot a male face waiting for them. If they have a choice at these moments, they will seek a female face at the register. However, they're not embarrassed to buy toilet paper, an item that deals with another bodily function which, theoretically, could be attended with feelings of embarrassment. But then we all, both males and females, defecate as a daily aspect of our lives, or at least we hope to. "It" doesn't suddenly appear during the tenth, eleventh or twelfth year of life. There is no mystery, no shame.

It's ironic that the standard for being "feminine" in our patriarchal society involves collaborating to eradicate any evidence of female sexual maturity such as a rounded belly, curvaceous hips and body hair. But then, such is the nature of war. Unfortunately, women have been co-conspirators in this battle against the feminine. Pubescent girls learn to battle against their bodies, fight the feminine within their selves. They defoliate, depilate and otherwise dilapidate their bodies, attempting to render them socially acceptable. While adolescence should provide opportunities for females to connect with the feminine within, it occasions further disconnection. We become our own worst enemies.

Tummy Talk

My mother enjoys telling a story about my brother as a child. Bananas were one of his favorite foods, and she teased him about his love for this fruit by playing a game. Whenever he ate a banana she pointed at his full little belly, normally more rounded after a meal, and joked about the banana sticking out of his tummy. They both enjoyed this little game.

One day my mother was invited to visit an acquaintance for tea, a social ritual in England. Deciding to take my brother with her, she cautioned him to be on his best behavior. They arrived at her friend's home and everything went smoothly until my brother marched up to the obviously very pregnant woman, pointed his finger at her belly and vociferously asked: "Is that a banana sticking out of your tummy?" The poor woman didn't know what to say. My mother, who might have been aware of the associative connection between bananas and penises, was very embarrassed. It was time to tell my brother about "the birds and the bees," that babies grow in mummies' tummies.

The associative connection between pregnancy, stomachs and food was not my brother's invention. It is a natural association, one that has been with us through the ages. There was a time when women were worshipped in recognition of their involvement in the creative process. This was before it was known that men contributed something, their sperm, to the act of creation. Women were associated with the creative source, Mother Nature, and the female form was idolized. Icons with large pendulous breasts, curvaceous hips, and protruding bellies were worshipped. Rituals recognized the feminine as the creative source, and social customs reflected this respect for female power, feminine energy.

After we learned of man's participation in the creative process and religious practices changed, the supreme evidence of femininity continued to be a curvaceous body with copious flesh. Women were encouraged to eat large quantities of food to attain this image. The heavier women in Rubens' paintings may seem repulsive by today's standards, but they were much admired.

Our attitude towards the female body, the feminine form, has changed. While women naturally have rounded tummies, we now expect them to be flat. We expect a woman to have a hard, angular, firm shape, even though her body is normally soft, with more fat content than a man's. Her greater proportion of fat is like a reservoir, an extra supply of energy available for a developing fetus.

During pregnancy, a woman's body becomes increasingly more feminine. While the internal changes are hidden, her breasts swell, her stomach protrudes and her hips widen. And as she grows rounder, fuller, softer, she often has mixed feelings about these physical changes.

I've discussed pregnancy with many women. In addition to talking with friends and colleagues, I've been privy to the innermost thoughts of my clients. These women use the sanctity of my office to shed pretensions and honestly explore feelings. They've taught me a great deal about how women experience their pregnancies.

One of my clients, "Judy," happened to have a session on the day she discovered she was pregnant. As she was feeling very confused, she took the opportunity to sort out her feelings. And while there was a part of her that was ecstatic, she was also worried and scared. She felt as if she were losing control over her body. Something else was taking over, and "it" was going to take charge of her body and control things from then on.

At first I thought Judy was talking about the baby, for every mother's life changes the minute she conceives. Her life is no longer her own, but shared with another being. This new life is someone who needs her constant care and attention, someone who totally depends on her. As I continued listening, I realized that Judy was also talking about something else.

Judy was talking about her body. "It" had developed a mind of its own, and she no longer felt in control. Her body had somehow conceived, and was now in charge of taking care of the baby's development, nurturing it, and watching over its growth. She didn't have a sense of this part of her self. It was a part she didn't know and didn't trust.

As I continued listening, I began understanding that "this part" was Judy's female part, her inner nature, the feminine. She had been battling "this part" for most of her life. No wonder she didn't have a sense of it, know it, trust it!

Judy was especially concerned about her belly. She had held a vague hope that therapy would ultimately lead to weight reduction. Now, instead of losing weight, she was going to be gaining, and instead of seeing her belly disappear, she would watch it growing. Moreover, she expected that her body would be permanently damaged, deformed. Pregnancy would leave its mark, stretch marks.

Even though Judy's emotions were uniquely her own, many women describe feelings similar to hers. Pregnant women typically express awe and amazement—incredulous that new life is being nurtured in their bodies. Some women are surprised to find themselves enraptured with the creative process. Yet along with this sense of wonderment, women also voice concerns about the future. While they discuss the responsibilities of having a child, and start preparing themselves for the shifts that will take place, many also express concerns about their bodies, about what has begun happening inside them. And they worry about becoming misshapen, unsexy, fat.

Society's battle with the feminine has been so successful that many women are unable to fully enjoy their pregnancies. While they may have difficulty naming the problem, they sense that something is wrong, bad, about "their condition." As pregnancy and birth embody the feminine, I'm no longer surprised that these processes have some undefined negative feelings attached to them. Women readily pick up on society's attitude towards the feminine.

According to Walker (1988), there used to be a custom, churching, which denied postparturient women admittance into church on the theory that giving birth made them spiritually impure. There was a quarantine period lasting for forty days if her baby was a boy, eighty if it was a girl. It was apparently twice as sinful to give birth to a girl. During this time both the woman and her new baby were officially designated non-Christian, heathen. At the end of this period the mother was expected to make an offering to the priest in atonement for her "sin." Even though our society no longer imposes these quarantines, it uses other, subtle tactics to ostracize the feminine.

The bulging belly is not only no longer revered, it is negatively associated with "fat." A woman's fear of becoming fat can distract her from focusing within. This keeps her from sensing the creative process, from feeling life stirring within, from connecting with the feminine.

Too many pregnant women feel ashamed of their protruding bellies. They try to tuck their tummies inside, and can't wait to get rid of them, back to their "normal" shape. Some are even tempted to diet, to battle with nature's plan for their bodies at this time. These attitudes toward our bodies are biased by an overly masculine perspective. In actuality, a woman's protruding belly is proof of her sexual prowess. It shows she is fulfilling her sexual mission, for she has conceived and is nurturing a child.

Contrary to masculine dogma, the sexual act does not culminate in orgasm and ejaculation. Although it is possible for a father to fulfill his obligation by contributing his sperm, the process of creating a new life is far from over. Pregnancy continues the process initiated by the sexual act. It is a process which reaches a climax in birth, and then moves on to the next phase.

Life is a continual process of creation and re-creation.

The process of creation is surrounded by mystery. Even though we attempt to understand, even imitate, this process, many of its secrets continue to elude us. Despite scientific exploration, it has retained its mythical mystique. It is nature's secret.

I see the process of creation as an interplay between masculine and feminine. They unite on many planes and many levels—from the cosmic to the molecular. It involves the spiritual and emotional, as well as the physical. Moreover, it takes place both inside and outside the female body.

The creative process starts with a mating dance. Masculine and feminine dance and weave around one another, moving closer and closer, then merge in a sexual act we call intercourse. This dance releases a messenger, a carrier of the masculine searching for the feminine.

Another mating dance ensues after a male sperm has found his way to a female egg. This dance reaches its climax when sperm impregnates egg, uniting with her to create a new life. This new life is a union of masculine and feminine, both aspects have contributed, both are present within it. This life is nurtured by the female, by her inner nature. She nourishes the composite of masculine and feminine that grows inside her. And then, when the time is ripe, rhythmic contractions push her fully formed child into the ocean of life waiting outside her body.

Pregnancy can be an opportunity to value the feminine, to recognize the part She plays in this cosmic drama of creation. Some women are able to take advantage of this opportunity, use it to connect with their inner nature. They tune in to their bodies and establish a relationship within their selves. It is a time, perhaps the first in many of their lives, when they are glad to be women.

These women recognize their important role in fostering life, promoting growth. Their inner environment nurtures the creative interplay between masculine and feminine. They feel creative. Some talk about feeling whole, complete.

I wish that every pregnant woman could glory in the creative life exploding inside her body. She should be proudly strutting around, delighting in her bulging belly, exhibiting it for the world to see. Instead, a pregnant stomach can be the site of a nine month battle, for as much as a woman may enjoy pregnancy, she often also strains against it. Her body is embattled territory in the war against the feminine. She is torn apart, separated from her center, her source.

Most of my clients describe their center as being located deep inside their bellies. Some identify it as being in the solar plexus region. Others find their center in the vicinity of the belly button. While the exact location may vary, time and time again my clients describe their center as being situated in the belly area. Oriental medicine similarly locates a person's energy center in the abdomen. They call it the "hara center."

I'm convinced that a woman's center is in her belly. Her power comes from here, from the earth within, her source of creative energy, the feminine. It is the soil of her self. However, when she is cut off from this source, from her femaleness, she looses touch with the feminine, her source of female desire, and is unable to feel wholly herself.

Many of my clients confess that they no longer feel sexual desire. While they remember feeling sexual during their younger days, they no longer experience these feelings. When they make love, they do so to please their mate, make him happy. They endure the proceedings without finding them pleasurable. And though they wish to feel close, they prefer a snuggling hug to a passionate embrace. They long for the passion they no longer feel.

Quite a number of my clients take these confessions one step further. They tell me they fake having orgasms. Their husbands or lovers care about them, want to give them pleasure, satisfy them. However, these women gain little pleasure from the activity, rarely experience the required orgasm, and resort to pretense to satisfy their mate and end the ordeal.

Sexual problems are complicated issues and I don't want to imply that there is any one simple solution. Nevertheless, one part of the difficulty stems from the way we think about sexuality. Our current concept is based on a masculine model. This model understands sexuality to be a drive with the goal of discharge. And while there is probably some truth to this model, the feminine aspect of sexuality may have additional twists. It's goal may not be the equivalent of masculine orgasm and ejaculation.

The creative interplay between masculine and feminine takes place inside a woman's body. Her body is built to nurture this interplay, sustain it, promote its growth. I suspect that this is the feminine aspect of sexuality—feeling, preserving, and nourishing the creative interplay between masculine and feminine. If this is the case, a woman's sexual nature is oriented towards sensuality, excitement, and passion more than discharge. Her pleasure comes more from the joy of dancing than the relief of music ending.

Sexuality may have masculine and feminine components, with males and females experiencing both forms, but each to a different degree. A woman's clitoris does "climax," and the birth process has parallels with ejaculation. These may represent the masculine dimension of a woman's sexuality.

Another aspect of this issue stems from society's commitment to continue repressing and suppressing the feminine. If a woman is at war within herself, battling the feminine, she doesn't have a chance to get to know her self, for she's too busy pushing her self away. Under these circumstances she can never know her desires, particularly in a world which says she isn't entitled to have any. As she's been battling with her body, she is, most likely, not fully present inside it. Any desire that might be there is lost, unavailable.

When a woman abandons her female center, her feminine source, she is cut off from desire, from passion, from experiencing the feminine. We have a great deal to learn about female sexuality, for women have been unable to fully experience their feminine selves, let alone express this aspect of their self. The feminine form of sexuality is unexplored territory. Our tummies are like the dark side of the moon.

Lost Voices

A client came to see me because she was having an affair. "Valerie" was married to a man she loved, but was obsessed with someone else. Even though she tried, she couldn't stop thinking about him.

Valerie wanted me to help her break off this affair, and was very surprised to hear me say that I didn't know if I would be able to help her end the relationship. She had tried to stop seeing this man, and wouldn't be in my office if it were that simple. The affair would already be over. I proceeded to tell her I suspected that the affair wasn't the problem. It was, more likely, a symptom of something else, an underlying issue. And while I didn't know what the issue might be, I suspected it would need to be addressed before she would be able to work through the symptom, give up her affair.

Valerie was flabbergasted. She didn't understand what I meant by "a symptom." All she knew was her preoccupation, her obsession. She couldn't stop thinking about him. Each time she severed their relationship, she was compelled to call him and tried to see him. She couldn't tear herself away from him. And I had the audacity to tell her he was "a symptom"!

Nevertheless, Valerie continued seeing me. Somehow she sensed that I knew what I was talking about. While she still didn't believe this man was a symptom, she trusted that I was going to be of help.

Our initial sessions focused on this man. I was one of the few people Valerie could talk with about him, for he was her secret. Gradually, we began exploring other issues, touching on her relationships with other men in her life, especially her father and her husband. After a while it became clear that whenever Valerie was angry, particularly with her husband, she began thinking about this man. It was at these times that she "couldn't resist" the temptation to pick up the phone and call him.

As we continued exploring other issues in her life, it became apparent that Valerie was avoiding her husband. She wasn't confronting him when she was angry. And she began understanding what I had meant when I said that her affair was a symptom. She recognized the connection between her anger towards her husband and her obsession with this other man.

Valerie continued the slow process of breaking free from her obsession. She gradually became more aware of her own issues, her own feelings, more in touch with her self. As her therapy progressed she was less inclined to hide behind her relationship with this man, more able to address her concerns, and deal differently with her anger. She became less preoccupied with him and saw him less frequently.

While I encouraged Valerie to go for couples therapy with her husband, she was afraid to begin dealing with him. It felt safer to avoid confrontation. She was also concerned that her secret might be discovered. It took over two years of individual therapy before she was ready to work on her relationship with her husband in couples therapy.

Again Valerie said good-bye to the other man. As difficult as it was, she stayed away. And when she was later put to the test, for they "happened" to meet, she was able to keep from resuming her relationship with him.

Even though Valerie was no longer involved with this man, I sensed she still had a wandering eye. She tended to focus on other men and obsess about what they were thinking and feeling. While she wasn't being unfaithful, I heard diluted versions of her previous obsession. When I shared my observation with her, wondering about what was happening, she was able to recognize that she was still looking for "something," a "missing piece."

Valerie began searching for the identity of this "missing piece." It didn't take long before she realized that the missing piece was inside her. She'd been looking outside herself to no avail. After this insight our work went in a different direction.

Valerie began focusing inside herself, listening for the voice of the missing piece. Once she began paying attention to what was inside, struggling to hear inner messages, she began connecting with her "missing piece." It was a long journey back to her self.

When Valerie first came to see me she was stuck in a self-perpetuating cycle. All my clients are stuck. They come into my office with symptoms—feelings or behaviors that are troubling them. Usually they've tried to work through these symptoms by themselves and seek me out because their attempts have been unsuccessful. Most of their symptoms have a repetitive, cyclical quality.

Symptoms are there for a reason. They serve a

purpose. Often they are unsuccessful attempts to solve a problem or a dilemma. As the issue itself doesn't get resolved, the symptom continues. My role, as a therapist, is to listen to clients' symptoms, hear their dilemmas, and understand their messages. Symptoms have a story to tell.

Symptoms exist because an important aspect of the self has been neglected—separated off, dissociated, repressed or suppressed. They are there to remind us that something has been dispossessed, disowned, lost. Symptoms contain lost voices that are crying for attention.

Valerie's obsession contained a lost voice—a part of her that kept trying to be heard. It wanted some attention. But as she was also committed to keeping that voice hidden, locked away, dissociated, she kept looking outside herself, unable to hear the voice inside. Her symptom became worse and worse, for the lost voice kept calling to her, trying to be heard. She was unable to hear it, and became stuck in a cycle, consumed by her symptom, hooked on a man.

Lost voices are hurt, wounded, disowned and dispossessed voices. As they are banished from the self and need to go elsewhere, they hide inside symptoms, waiting to be given an opportunity to speak, tell their stories, unfold their meaning. Their nagging voices keep repeating themselves, sending their messages, trying to be heard.

Lost voices find expression in physical and psychological symptoms. The lump in the throat, the knot in the stomach, the pain in the back, the headache, the stiff neck are all likely candidates for a lost and hidden voice. And while there may be physical reasons for these symptoms, there are often other, psychological reasons, why people have these problems.

"Beverly" came to me with a sharp, nagging pain in her side. She had been to a long list of physicians, subjecting herself to a series of physical tests and medical procedures, none of which showed any structural problem. Finally one of the physicians suggested that she speak with a therapist. And while Beverly persisted in her belief that something was physically wrong, she did come to see me.

Our initial sessions were devoted to lengthy descriptions of her pain. Beverly worried about undiscovered cancer—something was eating away at her side. After listening to the details of her physical complaints, I gently inquired into her emotional life. She described feelings of anxiety, pervasive panic, overwhelming fear. She was afraid to be left alone and had become an emotional cripple, constantly leaning on others. She was stuck in a cycle of pain and anxiety.

Having discovered that her father died shortly before the pain appeared, I suspected that issues surrounding this loss were contributing to her difficulty. Beverly was also the "typical female"—giving to others, unable to say "no" to important people in her life. And while she had a bubbly, cheerful, enthusiastic, life-of-the-party exterior, I sensed that other feelings lay hidden beneath this surface.

We began unraveling the mystery behind Beverly's physical pain. The knot in her side was a repository of feelings—sad feelings, angry feelings— feelings about her father—feelings about her experience of herself as a female in her family and in this society. These knotted up emotions sought expression and were given an opportunity to be heard. Words of anger, pain, humiliation, and sadness poured forth. And as she gave voice to her hidden feelings, listened to them, and valued them, her pain gradually diminished. Her feelings stopped needing a symptom to act as their mouthpiece.

People bring me their symptoms. They bring their depression, their anxiety, their fear, and their pain. Often they've waged a battle against these symptoms—tried to control them, fight them, get rid of them. Unfortunately, this approach perpetuates symptoms, and many people are stuck in self perpetuating cycles, struggling with symptoms that won't go away.

While anxiety is a symptom, people usually don't know how to hear the message encoded in this feeling. Instead, they develop behaviors for dealing with their anxiety. They try to get rid of it. Some of them "have to" avoid places, people or activities. These symptoms are called phobias. Others are compelled to approach, reach out, take in. These people have compulsions and addictions.

A compulsion is driven by an unconscious attempt to reconnect. It is a search for the lost voice, the lost part of the self, and consists of attempts to connect with what has been cut away, separated off from the self. The search is unsuccessful because it takes place in the wrong place—outside the person, rather than inside. In compulsions and addictions the search to reconnect is conducted outside, looking in the wrong direction.

We are a consumer oriented, addicted society—programmed to search for satisfaction outside ourselves. I see addiction as a symptom of our dissociated

world—as attempts to re-connect, re-member, re-asso-
ciate with that which has been lost, separated off, left
behind, forgotten. It is a search for a lost voice . . . Woman's Voice.

Woman's Voice

Woman's Voice is stifled—muffled by living in a masculine world with its his-story of repression and suppression. She is stuffed away, hidden in a secret place, shunted aside. We have lost the use of Her voice.

Woman's Voice is buried. She has retreated into mists where she hides in safety. Shrouded in mystery, she remains hidden—waiting to be discovered, waiting to be found.

Woman's Voice is not content with waiting. She makes her presence felt. For some, she is a nagging feeling in the pit of the stomach. Others may hear her in a sense of panic—seemingly coming from nowhere, overwhelming all else at the time. Her only way to express herself is through symptoms.

Woman's Voice is a lost voice. As her voice is not valued, but devalued, ridiculed and suppressed, she is disowned, dissociated, dispossessed. But she is still there—hiding. Symptoms are reminders that "something" has been lost. Woman's Voice is lost.

Associating

Connecting

Women are oriented towards caring and forming relationships. And while this feminine potential towards connection is often directed outside, towards other people, women can build on their capacity for connection. We can use it as a bridge to also connect with the feminine inside our selves.

A woman's relationship with the feminine is initially formed within the context of her family. And while I grew up in a patriarchal family, I am fortunate to have a strong mother—a woman who has a mind of her own, isn't afraid to express herself, voice her ideas, her opinions. My father delights in her feistiness, but generally ruled the roost.

My mother had been a relatively independent, "liberated" young woman. Even though women in her social position weren't supposed to work, she went against parental injunction and sought employment. Moreover, she moved to the city to be nearer my father during their dating years.

When my mother became engaged, she stopped working and returned to her hometown to prepare for her wedding. After her marriage, work was out of the question—"unthinkable." Then war intervened. My parents found themselves living in a topsy-turvy world. But while their assumptions about life were shattered and their lives uprooted, they were fortunate to escape from Hitler's clutches and land safely in England.

In England everyone was expected to work, contribute to the war effort. My mother, therefore, took a job in a department store until she became pregnant with me. Then she stopped working and reverted to the traditional female role. She became "housewife" and "mother."

My parents adhered to the traditional division of labor. We, the children, were considered my mother's domain. Yet, even with us, she alluded to his greater power and, as a last resort, occasionally invoked the ultimate threat: "Wait till your father gets home." This warning was used to buttress her authority. It had its intended effect, for we invariably cowered and acceded to her wishes.

While my father worked, sometimes traveling away from home on business, my mother tended the home fires. We appreciated her nurturing role, but looked up to my father, saw him as more powerful. It was only during her later years, once my brother and I were well off in high school, leading our own lives, that she resumed her creative endeavors. She became an accomplished potter.

My female role model was thus of a traditional woman. Any remnants of earlier dreams were projected onto us, her children. As she no longer imagined them for herself, she envisioned them for us.

Both parents supported my growth. They were generous with their love—encouraging me to pursue educational goals, supporting my desire to become a psychologist, and helping me fulfill my dreams. Nevertheless, they couldn't prepare me for my role as a pro-

fessional woman. As my mother didn't work and neither had her friends, I didn't have a role model.

When I first married I wasn't particularly concerned about combining my psychology career with
marriage. The two were compatible, for one didn't have
to be sacrificed for the other. But as time went on, I became uneasy, troubled by a nagging concern. Thinking
of starting a family was treading on unfamiliar waters,
and I wasn't sure I knew how to swim.

At first I couldn't articulate my apprehension, for I
didn't have anyone to talk with about this issue. Until I
met Connie, I didn't realize how hungry I was for another female role model—a female psychologist who
was happily married, worked, had children, did it all.
Connie taught a practicum in my graduate program,
and became my first female supervisor. As I was without a car, she occasionally gave me a ride home after
class. During these trips I plied her with questions
about how she managed to combine her home life with
a career.

Connie maintained her authority while genuinely
giving of herself. She told me that she never feels she is
doing enough for either her family, her students, or her
clients. Her honest answers were not only reassuring
at the time, but have also remained with me all these
years, reminding me that I am not alone in my many
moments of struggling with this issue.

Connie taught me more than she ever intended—
letting me know that a loving wife and mother could
also be an outstanding, competent professional
woman. Moreover, she showed me how to be a female
therapist, a therapist who could genuinely care, connect with other people, and yet remain free of entangle-

ment. She was grounded in her self.

When I later developed into an accomplished professional I began supervising other psychologists. A female psychology intern sought me out, asking if I would become her supervisor. Unlike myself at her age, she was able to articulate her needs. She wanted a female role model, a professional in her field.

It's no accident that we seek out female role models. Living in a masculine dominated society, we yearn for a feminine influence, the balancing aspect. We search for this dispossessed aspect of ourselves, hoping to find a way of connecting with the feminine, become whole, more complete.

Through relating with the feminine outside ourselves we begin daring to connect with the feminine within. This process of engaging with the feminine can take place in a variety of contexts. One of the most obvious places is in our relationships with other people.

Our relationships with others call upon the feminine aspects of our selves—our capacity for connection, empathy, and caring. We form many kinds of interpersonal relationships, and they should all be valued, protected and cherished, each for their own merits. Every relationship presents some possibility for expressing our feminine side. Something special happens when two people engage with one another in an intimate way. We travel deep inside ourselves, touching the depths of our own souls and connecting with someone else's. We open up parts of ourselves that are otherwise kept hidden, closed off, and locked away. By connecting with the feminine aspect of a cared for other person, we come closer to our own.

Friendships between women offer unique opportunities for affirming the feminine. Building upon shared female identities, we gather strength from supporting each other. These friendships are meaningful connections that validate the female voice.

Women often seek the company of other women as a way of supporting the feminine aspects of their selves. We do so individually and in groups. And while individual friendships appear to provide more intimate forms of connecting, the dynamics of a group add a particularly powerful element, the sense of female community.

A women's group enables its members to explore their feminine aspects and become rooted in this dimension of the self. Many women are pleasantly surprised by this process. For the first time in their lives they begin feeling comfortable with their female selves. As there are no social institutions which acknowledge, let alone affirm, the feminine, a women's group serves this important purpose.

Whenever the same group of women meets regularly, it gradually develops a life of its own that has a feminine identity. The group speaks with Woman's Voice. It can be a mother's group, a therapy group, a reading group, a quilting bee, or a gardening club. It is, however, important that the group be relatively small, preferably six to ten members, and that it meet on a regularly scheduled basis. As it takes time for members to trust one another and move into sharing personal aspects of their lives, the membership should also be consistent.

As group members gradually connect with one another, they tentatively risk talking about issues they usually keep to themselves and hide. Often they discover mutual feelings, shared concerns, communal anger, similar struggles with sexuality. They are affirmed by the group and in the group.

A women's group is empowering, for women gather strength from one another. Together they begin finding words, giving voice to that which is just below the surface but has no name, no face, until, with the power of the group, the face begins to emerge, and a name is found. They begin to face what is bothering them, face up to what they need to do, and come face to face with their selves.

For some, connecting with the feminine is a spiritual experience. These women, and men, have turned toward a spiritual representation of the feminine, the Goddess. This ancient tradition offers an alternative form of worship, one that values the neglected aspect. While women who choose this route may have individual ways of connecting with Her, they also join together in ceremonies, ritually commemorating the cycles of the moon, the seasons of the earth, nature's ways.

Therapy provides another context for connecting with the feminine. And while all therapists help people connect with dissociated aspects of their selves, I now feel that it is often useful for women to be in therapy with a woman. This is not because men can't be good therapists, some are intuitive, creative therapists, but because therapy is needed to heal wounds that are female wounds, incurred as a result of having been born in a female body in this culture.

A female therapist who is centered in her self and affirming of her womanhood, communicates this valuing of femaleness to her clients. She is also a powerful female with whom her clients can identify, someone who values the feminine way—the feminine sense of intuition—of thinking, feeling, acting, and doing—who knows in the pit of her stomach what it's like to be a woman. Her clients are enriched by being with such a woman. And by identifying with her, they begin connecting with Her.

I connected with the feminine through my relationship with nature. She became my therapist, offering me an opportunity to discover the neglected aspects of my self. This process began while our home was being built. I found my fingers itching to dig in the soil and nurture some roots, but our future home was surrounded by machinery. Trucks littered the area. Bulldozers were creating a cavern for our septic system, and other heavy equipment was drilling a well. A driveway was carved out of wilderness. Soil was laid bare. The land was raped—all under the guise of creating our future homestead.

As we had established our reign over land that had been wild, untamed and natural, somehow I knew that I needed to connect with the soil and try to make up for destruction we had caused. The land was beckoning and calling. She was crying out to me.

I yearned to plant, feel connected with a rhythm greater than my own, participate with nature, help her heal the land. And while I wanted the luxury of watching flowers bloom in grand profusion of color, I promised to learn from nature's ways and follow her path. When I vowed to return our land to a more natural state of being, little did I realize that I would be helped to discover my natural self along the way.

Even while we were building the house, I began adding a lilac here, an iris there, wherever I thought a

plant might be safe from the bulldozers. Then came the
time when I could safely plant. The machinery de-
parted, leaving barren land—bare soil crying for roots
to hold it in place and begin the healing process. I began tending Her garden by sowing seeds and setting
seedlings. And as I connected with Her, the seeds inside my self began to sprout, sending roots into my
earth within.

   Although I had intended to try healing the land,
the land offered something essential to my being. She
healed me. She offered me a way of turning inward,
connecting with myself.

   Reclaiming the lost voice, valuing the feminine
and entitling that voice, involves developing a relationship. The goal is to a-sociate, to get to know that which
has been dis-sociated, banished from the self. In this
society, it involves connecting with the feminine—ac-
knowledging, valuing, naming, and getting to know
Her in all the ways possible.

Entitling

Women are dis-entitled. We incorporate society's attitude towards the feminine and develop negative feelings about our selves. Our inner experiences are invalidated, our sense of abuse unnamed.

Naming grants recognition and confers an identity. Parents anticipating the birth of a child put a great deal of thought into a name. They sense the name is important.

Names contain information. They set an intention, create who we are, reflect where we've come from, and who we've become. However, there are often parts of our selves that remain unidentified, nameless. These are the disowned, dispossessed aspects of ourselves. As these parts don't have names it's impossible to communicate with them, learn anything about them. Healing requires identifying these dissociated, lost parts of the self.

In order to identify disowned aspects of ourselves, we need an inroad, a way of gaining access to the dissociated information. Usually this information is encapsulated in a symptom. And while people generally want to get rid of their symptoms, I recommend paying attention to symptoms, listening to them, hearing what they have to say. Symptoms are present for a reason, and they have a tale to tell. Sometimes their stories date back to traumatic childhood events.

When young girls are sexually abused they are frequently admonished not to tell. And as they don't tell, their experience of abuse is invalidated, their sense of abuse unnamed. Many years later they appear in my office as adults. They have a variety of symptoms, and may be depressed, have an eating disorder, or one of the anxiety disorders. Regardless of their presenting problem, they are usually out of touch with a whole part of themselves, the part that experienced the abuse.

Once we begin working together, exploring feelings, it isn't unusual for them to also describe feeling as if they have a lump in their throat, or some other physiological symptom. While this symptom serves a purpose, for a lump in the throat can prevent a lost voice from speaking, perpetuate the dissociation, keep Her from telling, it is generally also a doorway into the home of a lost voice. The symptom has access to the dissociated information.

When women begin listening to their symptoms they start connecting with dissociated aspects of their selves. They hear their own pain, suffering, agony, sadness, anger, rage. And they see the abuse. Those in therapy will describe something that happened to them, something they're ashamed to discuss, and if I use the word "abuse" in addressing the event, or events, they are always immensely relieved. As the word is the appropriate name for the event, it helps validate their experience, usually for the first time in their lives.

I've already mentioned "Claire's" breast reduction surgery. Claire was like many other women who have been blinded to their own abuse. It's kept unseen, hidden inside. An event, or events, is "forgotten" until a lost voice seizes an opportunity by rising to the surface, raising its voice, and demanding to be heard.

Claire initially came to see me because she was having marital problems and wanted to "sort things out" for herself. She was depressed and complained about her "weight," describing herself as having an "eating problem." In telling me about herself, Claire also mentioned that her grandmother had died during the previous year.

Our early sessions focused on Claire's lack of entitlement and her tendency to focus on pleasing other people. After being in therapy for quite some time, she began feeling more entitled to her own wishes and desires. She started being more assertive with her husband and also decided to have the breast reduction surgery. But while she felt "more daring ... and expressive" after the surgery, it hadn't resolved her difficulties.

We had never spoken of abuse. Shortly after the surgery Claire again mentioned her grandmother. She had warm, loving memories of her grandmother and had previously recalled that "she was always there ... was the only one who keyed into what I wanted." This time Claire began by saying that there was "a lot unresolved about Grandmother." Immediately afterwards, she began to cry, and described feeling "choked up." As we explored this feeling, Claire started having difficulty breathing and talking. She described a "weight" in her chest that was "round or oval ... heavy ... dark." Then she said "I can't escape," and further identified a "pressure at center of weight." This pressure was associated with "dominating ... fear."

This theme continued during later sessions, for Claire "remembered some fear." She tentatively began telling me about a "hidden area" and "blackness." The hidden area referred to her early years when she had been repeatedly abused by a group of boys older than herself. While she had not been raped, they physically forced her, and a few other girls, to submit to their wishes. They held her down and touched her, primarily in the vaginal area, but also sometimes around her breasts. In telling me about these events she said that she "felt a lot of guilt about it, felt it was my fault."

After discussing this "hidden area" Claire went on to address the "blackness." Her husband had also abused her. While his abuse was more mental, less physical, it was, nonetheless, abuse.

When we named these experiences, using the word "abuse," Claire breathed a long sigh of relief. After this physical release, her words flowed differently. She was no longer choked up. We discussed various situations of abuse that had taken place in her family. Neither she nor her husband had ever spoken of the abuse, but she now knew that she could talk about it and would find an appropriate time to do so with him.

Claire came in for her next appointment describing changes she'd observed since her last session. A major shift had taken place inside, for she now had the "power to say yes or no, or the power to say yes, but not now." She also no longer felt choked up, depressed, and anxious, but calm, at peace with her self. And, she could "think about Grandmother without being upset that she's not there."

I've recounted this therapy sequence because it exemplifies the process of entitling. Claire's sense of herself changed after naming the abuse. It was no accident that Claire had a "weight" in her chest and that she also had a problem with her "weight." This "weight" related back to the early abuse, and she had been carrying it around inside her since that time. Those boys had been throwing their "weight" around, pushing her down, forcing themselves on her chest. She'd been weighed down.

Like many other women, Claire had not trusted her inner experience. As it had been invalidated by other people, she had dissociated herself from her experience of "abuse," pushed "it" down, struggled to suppress "it." Entitling her inner experience, labeling it as "abuse," enabled her to stop pushing "it" down and start articulating her inner experience. She began listening to her symptoms, hearing what "weight" was trying to tell her.

We don't have to be in therapy to follow Claire's example of recognizing abuse, bringing it into the open, and naming it. The big step is to admit the abuse to ourselves, perhaps writing down instances when we've been abused. This kind of list tends to grow, for one recollection tends to prompt another memory, then another. And while it isn't necessary to talk about these experiences with someone, talking with another person such as a therapist, friend, colleague, or walking companion, can help confirm the abuse. Our inner experience of abuse is validated when we acknowledge that abuse has been "abuse."

Using the appropriate name, "abuse," helped validate Claire's inner experience. She was then able to address her dissociated part, the part that had been shut away, kept hidden inside for many years. This was a part she'd been suppressing, pushing down. And this part had been pushing back, raising Her voice, trying to be heard.

Claire's feelings about "Grandmother" opened the door to her memories of abuse and contained the key to her healing. "Grandmother" is a name that often symbolizes the feminine aspect—the discredited, and subsequently disowned, part of ourselves that has been denied a voice. Entitling Woman's Voice involves listening to Her, valuing the feminine aspect—our senses, feelings, and intuitions.

As representations of the feminine, feelings have become objects of social control. We've been taught to name feelings, not as a way of valuing them, but as a means of recognizing the enemy, controlling Her. And instead of welcoming all our feelings, statements such as "you shouldn't feel that way," suggest that feelings need justification, "good," logical reasons for existence.

Contrary to what we may have been taught, there are no "good" or "bad" feelings. We feel what we feel, and our feelings tell truths. However, many people confuse feelings with actions. They don't differentiate between having a feeling and acting upon it.

A feeling of wanting to hurt, harm, or even kill someone is a powerful feeling. It can also be a frightening feeling, for we may be afraid of acting upon it. But it isn't, in and of itself, harmful to feel this feeling. Only actions can actually hurt.

While there is a big difference between experiencing a feeling and acting upon it, there are times when one does lead to the other. As feelings don't just disappear or evaporate inside us, it can sometimes be dangerous to ignore them. Under certain circumstances, particularly if we pretend they don't exist, feelings can, and will, resort to action in their efforts to be heard.

Feelings contain important information. Recognizing our feelings, and hearing what they have to say, enables them to share their information. As this kind of naming moves a feeling along, it becomes part of a process and there is less of a tendency toward acting it out. It's more useful to value feelings and hear them, than to try and control or get rid of them.

When Claire had the breast reduction surgery, she was trying to get rid of her symptom, the heaviness in her chest, without hearing what it had to say. And while the surgery did physically reduce the "weight," it didn't address the underlying issue of how the weight came to be there in the first place. By listening to her symptom, Claire was eventually able to label her experiences as "abuse." Entitling the dispossessed parts of herself gave her a different kind of power, for by expressing her true feelings, she was finally able to get "'it' off her chest." The push came from inside, not outside.

While some feelings are reactive, responses to people or events in our lives, other feelings are proactive. They contain inner yearnings—our wants and desires. It's easy to lose touch with these feelings, particularly if we tend to focus attention outside our selves. Entitling our feelings includes listening to inner yearnings, valuing our wants, and expressing ourselves. We're all entitled to want.

Healing inner wounds involves valuing and empowering the dispossessed, disowned aspects of ourselves. As Woman's Voice is lost, she needs to be recognized, identified, acknowledged, given a name. Once this happens, She can be properly addressed, valued, and repossessed. Her voice can be empowered, encouraged to share Her information, put words on what She wants to say, participate in a dialogue.

If Woman's Voice is given an opportunity to share Her information, Her voice will move on. She will no longer be lost, and won't need to maintain residence in a symptom. Woman's Voice will then be able to grow, gain strength, continue to be heard, and contribute Her balancing aspect to the self.

Traveling

Lost voices speak a symbolic language, the language of dreams, fantasy and other reverie. Symbolic language is the language of the body. It speaks in pictures, smells, sounds, feelings, tastes—all forms of physical sensation. This language is more loosely connected, more associative, less logical. It's a metaphorical language where multiple meanings are woven together, merged within one symbol. There is no one true meaning, only meaningful connections of meaning.

Hearing a lost voice involves traveling down the inner path of association—taking an inner journey. This journey doesn't follow a straight, direct, logical path. Its route meanders around, following the trail of one association, then leaping along, or aside, to the next. It's a symbolic trail of hidden meanings and lost connections.

While therapy is one vehicle for taking this journey, traveling inside the self doesn't require the presence of another person. It does, however, require a safe space—a protected time and place within which the journey can take shape.

Creating time so that something can happen sounds easy, but is usually difficult, particularly for anyone who is at other people's beck and call. This tends to be the situation for many, especially women with children living at home. Nevertheless, it is essential to set aside some time. It's often necessary to schedule the time, make an appointment with one's self.

It also helps to have a quiet and peaceful place, a space that is protected from distractions that pull the attention outside. This space needs to be insulated from work, children, phone calls, whatever form an external pull may take. And while a closed door can be a blessing, a shield against those pulls, a safe place can be inside a car, or along a path while taking a walk in the woods. As long as the space is protected from outside intrusions it can become a safe space.

I had been writing this piece and took time out for lunch, planning to return as soon as my body was sufficiently nourished and my mind rested. While I was sitting, reading and eating, I looked up to see a friend standing outside my back door. As he could see me through the picture window, I felt obliged to invite him in and spend some time eating and chatting with him. Although I enjoyed his visit, this time had been carved out for myself—for my thoughts, listening to music, staring at drifting snow flakes. I felt slightly resentful it had been taken away. This is exactly the kind of situation to protect against when looking to take the inward journey of self discovery.

Writing has become one of the ways I travel inside myself. As my time is always full, I did some serious weeding to create some writing space. I made the commitment, gritted my teeth, perfected the art of saying no, and made the time.

When I came into the office this morning I knew I wanted to write about the inner journey. But in order to describe the process I needed to become more aware of it. I found myself starting to write, then stopping, sitting, creating a moment of inner silence, listening, waiting to hear what would speak from within.

I turned to face the window, sat staring into space. My gaze lost its focus. I wasn't paying attention to what was going on outside my window—though I did notice snowflakes falling, gracefully descending from the sky, as I began traveling down into myself.

I started the journey by drifting, floating, weaving from one association to another, following a trail of inner meaning. Each image flowed into the next until a pattern emerged, a form took shape. I followed this form, allowing it to lead where I needed to go. I floated down internal rivers, felt ripples, and heard a voice that magically appeared, unannounced, but welcome.

The snowflakes were still falling when I focused my eyes, reoriented, and found myself back in the office. I wrote the following in my journal:

I began by associating, traveling back in time, remembering earlier excursions into unknown territory. ... I'm walking along horsetrails, watching vegetation, noticing everything around me. There's so much to see, so much to smell, so much to feel. My heart resonates with the natural surroundings. I sense stillness around and within.

... Moving further back in time, I remember a faster paced activity, running. My legs are keeping a rhythm and the rhythm is keeping me as I travel round and around the same territory, following the same roads over and over again. And as I'm running, feeling the rhythm, the repetition of one foot moving in front of another, over and over and over again, I'm floating in time, weaving in and out, reflecting along the way.

... Then I'm outside our house digging the area destined to become my herb garden—digging for hours on end, resting here and there, staring into space, catching my breath, admiring my handiwork. The digging has a slow rhythm, lulling, soothing. My body feels alive. It has a purpose, a meaningful task.

My body shifts position. Digging becomes weeding. Senses awaken, as if from sleep. I'm listening to the silence. And I hear a voice.

A female voice is calling, using my names: "Lesley" ... "Irene" ... "Lesley" ... "Irene." Her voice has a haunting, compelling quality. I want to run to her, find her, embrace her. There's no holding back.

... I'm in a forest, surrounded by green, running through underbrush. Trees rise high above my head. Shrubs and tall grasses whip and scratch my legs. Her voice keeps calling.

... And I'm searching through caves, scurrying from one to the next, reaching for the voice. I'm in a labyrinth, an underground maze.

... There's fog in the distance. Her voice grows louder, more distinct. I feel as if I'm getting closer.

Then, suddenly, I hear another voice, a man's voice. He too is calling, but pulling in another direction. I'm torn—betwixt and between.

The male voice grows insistent, more demanding. There's a loud knocking on my office door, summoning my attention, ending this particular journey.

Returning to my desk, I reflected on my travels. I recognized that outdoor, nature oriented, solitary activities had helped me focus inside. In the quiet of nature I heard my own thoughts. They weren't drowned out by static. And I could hear Her calling.

Traveling is opening to inner space, then listening, hearing inner messages. Although I never know where the journey will lead, it always begins with a moment of stillness, then shifting attention, and focusing inward. This shifting of attention inward is going into a trance, an altered state of consciousness. And while I hesitate to use a word that conjures up all sorts of associations, I use the word "trance" because it best describes the inner focusing of attention.

I went into a trance the moment I began staring at the snowflakes outside my window. My attention initially narrowed, then began finding internal spaces for its journey. There was an emptying of thought, an openness to internal messages.

While exploring inner terrain cannot occur while with other people in the usual manner of face-to-face relating, anything that directs attention towards the self can facilitate trance. A properly phrased therapist's question accomplishes this task. Repetition and rhythm also induce this state by lulling our vigilant senses to sleep. Attention can then shift, move into other terrain.

The rhythmic movements in running, walking, digging and weeding quietly rock me into myself. These activities help me focus inside, begin listening and hearing. And while their solitary nature is essential, there are many ways of moving inward. Some of these ways use the breath to initiate the traveling process. These centering and meditational techniques are described in later chapters.

It's a fallacy to think of trance as a magical state induced by a hypnotist's wand. While it does have a certain magic, it is a place we enter many times a day.

Most people are familiar with this place, for it's where our daydreams take shape.

... You're driving your car, and the rhythmic sound of wheels turning, the rocking of the car, and the road continually moving, are casting a spell. Without realizing it, you're lost in reverie and arrive at your destination unaware of having driven there. Your mind and body drove to your intended destination, while your consciousness traveled inward, freely roaming along inner roads and pathways.

Or, have you ever rocked or walked an unhappy infant, hoping to soothe the child? If so, perhaps you've noticed the quieting effect of this repetitive and rhythmic activity. Not only does the baby become calm, peaceful, perhaps go to sleep, but you may also have noticed the effect it had on you, the calming mood this activity calls forth, and a shift of awareness during this process, perhaps feeling more centered inside your own body.

Rhythmic movement, repetitive motion, and time by ourselves create space to associate, to mull, to tune out the irrelevant and tune in the relevant. When we enter this quiet, peaceful place inside ourselves we travel into another world—a world paved in symbols, associations, multiple meanings.

Entering into a trance is a way of creating inner stillness. It is a precursor of other shifts, creative internal moments, change. Lost voices are heard in this stillness.

Transportation

The inner journey is a voyage into uncharted territory. This uncharted territory is abandoned land. It is inhabited by lost voices—disowned and dispossessed aspects of our selves.

There aren't any marked roads leading to homes of lost voices. After years of disuse weeds begin to grow, making whatever roads were there increasingly difficult to negotiate. Roads become paths. Then the paths almost disappear, becoming hidden in the undergrowth beneath the trees and between the brambles.

As these paths are almost inaccessible, they cannot be traveled on foot. A vehicle is needed to negotiate the difficult terrain. And while many journeys require vehicles, this one requires a special type—one equipped for our inner terrain.

We're all familiar with vehicles that ride on the surface of a road, in water, and through the air. Many of us know how to pilot these vehicles. We know how to ride a bicycle, or drive a car. But we're less familiar with forms of transportation available for traveling inside ourselves.

While therapy can serve as a vehicle for the journey, the voyage itself is a solo flight—a solitary expedition into inner space. Excursions into dreamworld are such flights. Travel is weightless, plunging into inner depths, and soaring toward outer limits of our selves.

At night we are safely encapsulated in the womb of sleep. During daylight, our daydreams take shape within the protective web of trance.

Even though we may not remember many of our dreams, we all use this vehicle for traveling inside ourselves. Lost voices speak to us in dreams. They're usually disguised, but they are there, waiting to be heard.

As I rarely remember my dreams after fully awakening, I leave a pad of paper and a pen next to my bed. They're positioned so I can readily find them without needing to turn on the light. Sometimes I write down the content of a dream, but more often I jot down twilight associations, dream meanings that come to me while only half awake. I never know when that pen and paper will come in handy, but they did just the other night.

I had been having difficulty starting this piece. As sometimes happens, I sat down at the desk and immediately felt like getting up again. I wanted to eat. At first I fought this urge, battled with my self. Then I realized that battling never leads anywhere constructive. I decided to have something to eat, expecting I would then be able to resume my work. When I returned to my desk I wrote a few words, and then experienced another urge to get up and eat. This kept happening all afternoon and evening.

While eating can be pleasurable, I didn't enjoy this way of eating. I hadn't savored the taste of the food. Even worse, I didn't feel nourished. Rather than listen to my body, nurture it, I had been oblivious to its signals. And while I consoled myself that I had consumed healthy food, I had eaten far too much, felt uncomfortable, and had been eating for the wrong reasons.

By the time I went to sleep there were two issues preying heavily on my mind. I was still struggling with my writing problem. And I was troubled by my eating, wondering what it meant. Although I don't remember whether I had been dreaming, I woke up in the middle of the night and began to write. The next morning I deciphered my scribbles. A sentence read: "Some vehicles don't have the power to travel to lost voices." Then there was another note. It merely said "free associate."

I immediately understood that the sentence referred to my eating the night before. Compulsive behaviors, like eating, don't have the power to lead to a lost voice, a hidden meaning, an inner message. These vehicles loop around, get stuck in a cycle, stay in a rut. And while eating didn't have the power to take me where I needed to go, the technique of free association is well equipped to negotiate the paths of inner space.

Freud introduced the concept of free association. He directed his clients to allow their thoughts to emerge uncensored, to express whatever comes to mind. While free association is primarily considered a therapeutic technique, there are other ways of applying it. Writing can be a wonderful way to free associate. I often encourage people to keep a journal, write down their thoughts, images, feelings, sensations—journey into their selves. I'd been forgetting to use this vehicle with myself.

My morning scribble reminded me to free associate on paper. As soon as I could, I went to my desk and began writing, putting down anything and everything that came to mind. I avoided thinking about what I was writing, allowing whatever emerged to travel directly down my arm, through my fingers, to the paper. After a

lot of gobbledygook, I found myself writing about
"Mary."

Mary came to me after an automobile accident.
She was lucky to survive the accident, managing to
regain the use of her body through courage, determination, and extensive surgery. However, she was in pain.
And while most of her pain was due to these injuries,
she was hoping to learn psychological techniques to
help her deal with it.

Despite all her physical problems, Mary led a
busy, active life. She worked in a hospice program,
assisting cancer patients in whatever way she could.
She was also very involved with her church, tending to
assume responsibility for many of its functions. However, there were times when she was unable to function, for she became paralyzed with pain, and had to go
to bed.

Listening to Mary's story I recognized that her
symptom, her pain, was telling her something. By forcing her to lie down and take it easy, it was trying to tell
her that she needed to take time away from attending
to other people's needs and begin paying attention to
herself. Perhaps if Mary could hear what her symptom
was telling her, she would find another way of giving
herself what she needed.

As tension gets transmitted to muscles, magnify-
ing existing pain, I began teaching Mary a variety of
relaxation techniques, from progressive muscle relaxation to modified meditation. At first she had difficulty
using these techniques. As she was focused outside
herself, she had difficulty traveling inside. Then I discovered that she enjoyed music. Mary sang in her
church choir and loved listening to classical music. But

she was so busy running around taking care of other people that she rarely had time for the simple activity of sitting and surrounding herself with music.

I suggested that Mary schedule a time each day to turn on her music and tune into herself. At first she resisted the idea, for she had lead an active, committed life prior to her accident, and was disinclined to begin "pampering" herself. But as she loved listening to classical music, she gave it a try.

Listening to music transported Mary into a space inside herself where she could hear her own messages. Once she paid attention to these messages she heard that her body had been asking her to take time off to relax and lie down. And even though Mary's pain never totally disappeared, she was able to reduce the frequency and severity of her pain by regularly taking time to listen to "her music."

While music was Mary's vehicle, each person has their own way of traveling inside. Most of my clients learn to recognize and take advantage of their particular vehicles. While some of them run or take walks, others meditate or make bread. A few keep journals. Others paint. And a number of them listen to music, with some also playing one or more musical instruments.

Sometimes vehicles are tailor-made, designed to suit a particular terrain. "Judy" rearranged her whole house, placing a comfortable chair in each room where she could be with "Green," the name she gave to the peaceful place within herself. Sometimes she reads in one of these chairs. At other times she just sits. These chairs serve as her vehicle, and are an important part of her life.

While each of the activities I've been mentioning can be inherently pleasurable, enjoyed for itself, they are also ways of traveling inside the self. I never give assignments or prescribe any of these activities, but I do encourage them. I support any creative endeavor that involves receptivity, opening to inner space. Creativity is a key to communicating with a lost voice.

In my experience, all the "arts" provide a form of transportation as well as a medium in which Woman's Voice can be heard. Woman's Voice speaks a somatic language, a language of the body. She uses feelings and other sensations as Her way of communicating. These are the kinds of perceptions expressed in art.

Creativity taps into the feminine, gives Her a form for expression, a voice. It weaves masculine with feminine, right brain with left brain, and feeling with form. As artistic productions call upon the feminine aspects of our selves, these vehicles are particularly equipped for the journey to Woman's Voice. But we must refrain from judging the artistic merits of our "work," for adopting an attitude of play helps engage the lost parts of ourselves.

Even though one person's vehicle may not be suited to another's inner terrain, everyone has a form of transportation they can use. Each person needs to discover their own vehicles, experiment until they find ways that work for them. Writing works for some people and is their preferred way to travel. It helps me listen to my inner voice. I hear words, put them on paper, then take them in with my eyes. I listen with my internal ear, see with my outward looking eye. It's like being in therapy with myself, looking at my self in the mirror.

I also investigate other practices, and one such experiment was with meditation. As I'd heard a great deal about the benefits of meditation, I took a few workshops on different approaches, then signed up for a course. I learned how to sit in a still but comfortable position, then breathe in, follow the breath to my center, and remain there watching the breath as it moved in and out, and in and out, focusing all my attention on the breath. When my mind naturally began wandering, I gently brought it back to the breath.

I diligently practiced the sitting meditation, learning how to still my self, become centered in myself. While I valued knowing how to use my breath this way, my experience didn't match the glowing reports I'd heard from other people. This form of meditation gradually slipped out of my daily routine.

I had a similar experience with visualization. Whenever I tried to take a visual journey, either creating my own hoped for scenario, or following someone's specific instructions, I generally had difficulty seeing clear images. While other people described vivid pictures, I never saw pictures—only vague images interspersed with thoughts and other sensations. At first I blamed myself, felt inadequate, and thought I was doing it incorrectly. Then I gave up trying to duplicate other people's experiences and began appreciating my own. I stopped trying to visualize.

Having heard experts extolling the virtues of meditation and visualization, I was surprised by my response. While they were touted to be universal vehicles, walking and writing felt more effective for me. I puzzled over this paradox, wondered about it on my walks. It began making sense when I realized that my primary sensory modality is the kinesthetic pathway.

According to neuro-linguistic programming, people have preferred modes for processing information. Our bodies are equipped with a variety of sense organs, each of which is constantly engaged in processing information. And while we are all generally capable of seeing, smelling, hearing, tasting, and feeling, we tend to favor some modalities over others. In addition, we store information using the form in which it was processed. Our words reflect the modality in which we process and store information.

Some people store information in visual containers. They tend to use visual words, asking questions such as: "Can you *see* what I'm getting at?" While they may describe someone as being *bright*, a *shining* star, people who rely on other modalities tend to choose different words.

The person who says "That *sounds* good to me," has used the auditory channel for processing the information. Someone else might say "I can just *taste* what it would mean to become successful," or "that was a *bitter* pill to *swallow*," using gustatory language to describe their experience. Then there are those who rely on olfactory messages when "*smelling* a rat," or "*sniffing* out a problem."

A client yesterday talked about wishing her husband would "*hear* her." When I offered some advice she stated "that *sounds* like a great idea." As she didn't say "I *see* what you mean," I suspect she favors the auditory modality.

Although I process some information visually, I favor the kinesthetic mode. I tend to talk about "*feeling* things" and "*sensing* something happening." As walking is a kinesthetic activity, it's no wonder that I've come to rely on it as a vehicle for self-exploration. My information is primarily stored in kinesthetic forms.

I suspect that the forms of transportation for traveling inside ourselves are tied to our sensory modalities. As I'm more kinesthetic, movement is likely to serve as my vehicle. People who favor the visual modality might be better off using visual vehicles such as visualization and painting.

Some vehicles combine sensory modalities. Sculpting, potting, basket making, and gardening are vehicles that utilize kinesthetic as well as visual cues. People who gravitate towards music probably use both auditory and kinesthetic cues.

Many people, especially clients seeking therapy, know that their vehicles haven't been working properly. When our vehicles get stuck in a rut, it's usually because of the fuel we've been using. We've usually been looking outside ourselves for fuel. In contrast, an empowered vehicle is one that derives its energy from inside, from the body, from the belly. This energy is creative energy. The fuel comes from within.

It isn't easy finding a pathway to a lost voice. Once the pathway is found, like other paths, it needs to be used. And as it's used, it becomes easier and easier to locate. It's important to continue using this pathway, keep it open, have it become an open channel for communication, for a-sociation.

The path of association leads towards a lost voice. It travels through the land of hidden meanings and sensory messages. It's never a direct path, and getting lost is an important part of the journey. We usually get lost before arriving at a doorway, an entrance to the home of a neglected or suppressed voice. It's in the art of getting lost that discoveries are made.

Lost

When I sit down to write, I begin with a sentence or two. Then fog moves in. The words don't seem right. And, as fog grows nearer, sending wisps of gray in my direction, the words grow hazy. Their edges blur, gradually, till there are no edges. After the period comes another, and another, and another. I'm lost.

My mind is blank. I want to get out of the chair, make a phone call, move, travel, try to find something, anything. I begin searching, trying to find my way—my body moving in all directions, seeking a landmark. However, it's the internal landmarks that are missing. My mind is as restless as my body.

Thoughts begin to whir, going round and around in an endless circle. Thoughts circling around—a jumble—a fog all around—swirling, moving. Movement that leads nowhere and everywhere all at once—in all directions and no direction. Repetitive movement where nothing seems right, nothing feels right. I'm lost in a sea of circling words, circling ideas—a vortex of circles, pulling me down—a heaviness.

The heaviness starts in my chest. "Oh, no, I'm lost." A panicky heaviness that's pulling me down, down, further down, down to ...

And I'm back in time, sitting on the corner of a curb, my bicycle nearby, lying on the ground. A scrape on the knee. Tears trickling, then rolling down my

cheek. I'm unable to move one way or another, frozen
on the curb, unable to see in any direction—stuck on
the curb with a sad, frightened, heavy heart that
pounds, that yearns to pound the pavement and
scream. But no sounds echo forth.

I look in one direction, then another. Sitting, all
alone, frozen, unable to move. Glued to the corner,
stuck, cornered, unable to turn the corner, stuck between here and there. Lost.

The world's an endless sea of unfamiliar places.
Looking to the right, looking to the left. I'm left. I'm
alone, all alone, alone with heavy, not my Teddy, just
heavy, heavy heart. Oh where's my Teddy? Is Teddy
lost too?

And heavy heart pounds and pounds. And it
pounds. Oh the weight of those pounds. Keeping time
where there is no time. I'm lost—lost in time and lost in
space. There is no place, only space, endless space. Fog
and mist. Missing and missed.

Where's my mommy? Where's my daddy? Missing.
Missing people, missing places. Losing people, losing
places. Lost. All is lost. I've lost my way.

Like that time with mummy when we were lost.
The fog came in slowly, creeping, softly. There was no
sound, only movement. It came rolling down the hill,
tumbling over itself, and over and over and over itself.
Gray swirls, moving—always moving—eating one
house, then the next. Stealing upon them. And one by
one they disappeared—swallowed by fog—lost. Swirling, coming stealthily—till we were surrounded by
gray—whirling gray movement—no form, only gray.
At times an outline appeared to take shape, then disappeared, moved into the distance behind gray.

The mist, the missed and the missing merge. It's one fog, a fog of spiraling, swirling feeling—confusion—searching. Searching for all that's been lost—not my loss, but our loss, shared losses.

And as I journey to unfamiliar places, becoming lost gets more familiar. I get acquainted with shapes and faces in the fog. Images grow clearer, take a form, a shape, a name. The gray begins to lift as some light pushes it away.

The light spreads, becoming a sheet of light shining on the curb. Then the curb elongates, extends its reach, and grows into the path of light. There's a sense of direction, a place to go.

At first I follow the curb, turning the corner. And as the fog continues to clear, the light shines brighter. The sheet becomes a page. Letters form. Words appear. I can sit down and write.

I found Her voice.

Voice

I am the voice, the buried voice, the voice that was gassed and muffled, till there was almost no voice. I have been shut away—hidden, lost. Lost, but I will be heard. The time has come for my voice to reverberate.

I am Woman's Voice, the voice of the Grandmother, the feminine. I arise from the earth and my voice will take root in the hearts and souls of men and women. I will be heard.

And as I am heard and give voice to my concerns, I will have power—a different kind of power. This power comes from my belly, from my womb, my womanness, from my connection with creativity, with female energy.

My voice speaks of wholes, of connections, the power of "And." For I am you. We are one. We are one voice.

I am your voice. We are born in the womb of woman's body. It is time to be born, to become whole. A different birth—not a rendering into separateness, but a connecting into wholeness.

I offer myself as your teacher, your guide. You can find me in the form of a symptom, a visual image, a sound, a smell, or a feeling. I live in the inner circle— the place from where knowing comes—the place that's the beginning of being—the beginning of being with your self.

Dig down deep and you'll find me.

Healing

Wise Women

Woman's Voice is my voice
She's your voice
She's all our relations

My parents enjoy visiting Harmony Farm. Sometimes they come in late summer, the time of abundance. Blueberries are ripe, demanding to be picked. The vegetable garden is bursting with color, making its annual offering of many gifts. And, in the woods, the mysterious mushroom is poking her head above ground. Nature is in her glory.

I have vague memories of mushrooming in England. These family excursions were long forgotten until my mother began taking leisurely walks through our woods, scouring the floor for mushrooms. One day she triumphantly returned with some valuable treasures, a handful of mushrooms. She excitedly showed her discoveries to my husband and I who looked at the foreign brown beings with suspicion. As we were only familiar with the white, cultivated variety, these other specimens seemed alien. We wondered if they were safe, hesitated to touch them.

Our obvious distrust of this wild food put a damper on my mother's excited enthusiasm. She hadn't been raised in the area and couldn't absolutely guarantee she'd correctly identified the mushrooms.

Even though they were "just like the ones from home," we didn't eat the mushrooms.

The next year brought books. Our Christmas stockings were stuffed with a series on mushroom identification. These books were tailored to our area and included beautiful colored photographs, as well as detailed descriptions. While now ostensibly well prepared for future mushrooming events, we also read some articles about wild mushrooms. These articles detailed the dangers of eating the mysterious mushroom, warning of toxins lurking within, disguised, waiting.

My mother continued to visit and roam about the woods. During mushroom season she couldn't resist bringing some back to the kitchen, hoping I would eventually recognize their worth. The abandoned identification books were rescued from their dusty places on the shelves, as she painstakingly perused their contents to insure the safety of her finds. My husband and I suspiciously looked back and forth, from picture to real life, hesitant, frightened, and unsure. The unfortunate mushrooms landed on the compost pile, where at least they could do some good.

This pattern continued for many years. Eventually my mother gave in to our skepticism. She stopped picking mushrooms.

But the mushrooms continued in hot pursuit, tracking me down in my favorite restaurants. These restaurants began offering wild mushroom delights, awakening my taste buds to their unique and delectable flavor. Then they followed me into the woods, appearing on my walks, surfacing along the trails. They seemed to be watching, keeping an eye on me, as they mysteriously appeared, then disappeared. They were beckoning, teasing, flirting.

Our frequent meetings aroused my curiosity. I began wondering which ones might be safe to eat, hoping to eventually recognize them, distinguish between them. The mushrooms were finding their way into my heart. I wanted to get to know them.

Again my parents came to visit. This time they brought a relative, my mother's cousin Liesl, who was visiting from England—someone I hadn't seen since my youth and barely remembered. We had a spirited family reunion, one that occasioned many forms of connecting.

Our first evening was spent getting acquainted, communing around the dinner table. We rapidly moved to common ground with each other. I felt drawn to my "aunt," sensed a kindred spirit, and began tapping into my roots.

Later that evening calamity struck. Something happened with the water pump to our well and we no longer had water. What were we going to do with a houseful of guests and no water? They wouldn't be able to brush their teeth, let alone use the toilet, or take a shower.

My father immediately solved the problem by offering to go to a hotel the next morning. As I'd looked forward to a weekend of sharing our life with my relatives, I wasn't willing to give up that easily, and began searching for other solutions. Then, remembering that a new local supermarket would still be open, I ran off to buy water.

On the way to the store my mind was racing, speeding ahead to solve our water problem. While I would probably be able to buy water to drink, what would we do about other essentials? My mind went round and around searching for solutions. There would be food to prepare, dishes to wash, and activities to perform around bodily functions.

Then, I remembered our pond—a natural body of water on our property. How could I have overlooked this resource, even a shallow, muddy one? Our problems wouldn't be solved, but we were on the road to being able to live with this "disaster." Water from the pond could readily be used to flush toilets, soak dishes, even cleanse a perspiring body.

After purchasing ten gallons of water for morning rituals including the necessary cups of herbal tea, I began my journey home. By this time I'd become philosophical. The essentials would be handled. A lesson could be learned.

This experience was teaching me the value of our pond. I'd been appreciating its beauty, but taking it for granted, and had never graced its waters with more than a foot or a hand. Perhaps this "disaster" was one of nature's gifts, an opportunity to change my relationship with our pond.

My husband had similarly recognized the pond's potential and early the next morning brought buckets of water for each of the bathrooms. However, my mother had another solution—with toilet paper in hand she headed for the woods. My father and "aunt" soon followed suit, refusing to take advantage of the modern amenity, claiming that my husband did not need to bring water for them. My parents, aged 75, and relative, in her early 60s, were each determined to prove they could survive without modern plumbing.

Everyone was in a good humor. While they hadn't expected to truly live in the woods, they were enjoying this respite from city life. The toilet paper was ceremoniously placed in a basket near the door, ever ready for nature's call. My father even returned from one "visit to the woods" extolling the virtues of the squat position. It had been "good exercise."

Having completed our morning ablutions, we sat down to breakfast, then more visits to the woods. My mother returned from one such visit, excitedly declaring there were mushrooms to be had. She brought a prize specimen back, and invited us to each take a whiff. When I put my nose in its vicinity I was transported to the woods. It was saturated with smells of earth, leaves, and trees.

My mother and her cousin made immediate preparations for a mushroom hunting expedition. This time I was eager to be included. We set out with baskets and knives. The knives would be used to cut the mushrooms, ensuring that their roots stay in the ground, enabling future propagation.

While our feet meandered through the trees, our eyes busily scanned the forest floor. Meanwhile, my mother and her cousin journeyed back in time to similar occasions in their youth. They began to reminisce about growing up in their homeland, Czechoslovakia, their shared relations, and similar family excursions.

We managed to locate quite a few specimens. Each time one of us spotted a possibility, the others scurried over. My mother and her cousin continually checked with each other to confirm the mushroom's identification. Sometimes they merely glanced at a mushroom, noted its color and passed it by. Other times they looked underneath to see if it had gills. If my mother suspected a mushroom to be poisonous she tended to use her shoe, tipping the mushroom on its side with the tip of her foot. Whenever she believed it to be a tasty, edible morsel, the knife was called into play and the stem skillfully sliced.

Sometimes the mushroom was brought towards the nostrils, and its essence inhaled to further clarify its nature. They used the names from their youth, not the botanical ones in my various books. I learned that mushrooms were named according to their habitats. For example, ones that were typically found under birch trees, "birken," were called "birkenpilze."

While my mother and her cousin readily identified many of the mushrooms, others were not familiar to them, having not been indigenous to their homeland. Throughout this process I was all eyes, ears and nose, eager to absorb their knowledge, the information that had been part of their heritage, their youth. I was being initiated into a whole new world—a world that was new to me, but full of old wisdom.

These women in my life, my lifeblood, were introducing me to another way of knowing. This wisdom has been hidden, submerged in our culture which distrusts nature, and values the cultivated mushroom over those found in the wild. I wanted to enter their circle, and learn all I could about that ancient wisdom before it is lost to all of us.

I began thinking about this knowledge. It wasn't the domain of country folk, for my mother and her cousin had lived in a sophisticated, urban area. Similarly, it didn't belong to the poor and uneducated, for they had grown up among the educated elite. Neither did it belong purely to women, for men could also be knowledgeable in these ways. It was a "woman's way" of knowing—a bodily way of knowing practiced by "wise women."

Having heard a grumbling in our stomachs, we headed back toward the house, baskets brimming with various prizes. Arriving in the kitchen we sliced the mushrooms, making sure that none turned blue, then discarded parts that had been graced with a worm or other foreign creature. Rather than put them to immediate use, we decided to preserve them for a future meal. They would dry in the sun.

My mother recalled days of drying mushrooms on newspapers, but as I was wary of ink, we agreed to use trays of a modern convenience, an electric food dehydrator. If the mushrooms weren't dry at the end of the day, rather than expose them to the dampness of dew, we could finish them off in the dehydrator. The mushrooms were ceremoniously placed in position atop a large rock in the sun.

Lunch was primarily gleaned from our garden. A fresh salad of wild and cultivated greens, tomatoes, cucumbers, carrots, beets and herbs. Fresh whole grain bread came out of the oven, and some store bought smoked salmon and goat cheese completed the meal. It was a sumptuous feast, an overflowing table— delightful colors gracing our eyes, delectable aromas wafting into our nostrils.

The family reassembled around the table. Food was passed from one to the other. We were all hungry, eager to eat, and savor the tastes. Our conversation circled around the morning events as well as our other preoccupation, water. We were each valuing water, appreciating every drop that went into our mouths or down the sink. Sometimes we forgot and automatically went towards the faucet, only to hear its empty hiss, and remember our plight.

Despite our water limitations, we managed to clean up after our meal. We were using other resources, finding solutions to each dilemma as it arose. Luckily the sun was shining and our "visits to the woods" were taking place in good weather—an opportunity to enjoy being outdoors. Life felt good.

My mother, her cousin, and I had formed a circle. We were weaving in and out with one another, separating for one task or another, then rejoining the circle. Our connection deepened as each new thread was added, as we wove together through the day.

After lunch we took our circle to the fields where wild blueberries were ripe and waiting. As we picked and talked I watched my mother and her cousin. Both had smiling faces, though one with more lines than the other. I felt warmth emanating from each, then surrounding the other. Here we were, three of us, with vast age gaps, yet bridging differences, and sharing an experience. I rapidly calculated and realized that there were approximately 15 years between myself and my mother's cousin, and another 15 between the two of them. It was as if we spanned three generations of women.

The pump repair people finally answered our call, and sent someone to the rescue. He managed to replace the defective part, and we cheered the sound of gurgling water surging forth from the faucet. Our glee was tinged with respect. In less than a day we had gained a new perspective. While we were thankful for the mod-

ern convenience of plumbing and pumps, we had come
to value nature's resources, especially water. Our excursions into the woods with the basket of toilet paper
will forever be etched in our minds.

After mentally thanking the pond for having
shared her resources with us, I opted for the luxury of a
steaming hot shower before dinner. We traveled to a
local restaurant in good cheer, feeling cleansed inside
and out. There my mother and I both "happened" to
order a wild mushroom appetizer, which we shared
with the others. One sharing led to another, and we
were soon talking about a myriad of other events. Our
female circle easily expanded to include the men.

My parents and "aunt" journeyed back to their
youth, somehow circling around to their mothers, their
grandmothers, then back to themselves. The discussion focused on their upbringing, the upbringing of
women in their era. Even though their families had
been wealthy, neither my mother nor her cousin had
been educated in a profession. When my mother re-
belled and sought employment, she was admonished
for having taken a job away from someone who might
have needed it.

My father was part of the discussion, for he had
lived in their community, grown up in that world. Their
mothers lacked meaningful work, for they had servants to do their housework, their cooking, cleaning,
and caring for the children. There was little to give
meaning to their lives. My mother's mother, an accomplished pianist with two grand pianos and a small or-
gan in her home, looked to her music. Other women
resorted to having affairs as a way to escape boredom,
feel important, and enliven their lives. Their talents

weren't recognized or valued.

As I listened to the discussion going round and around, I was thankful for my inheritance. In contrast to these earlier generations, I had been given opportunities for growth, a career, and meaningful work. My grandmothers and mother paved the way, one rebellion leading to another, and here I was, now, benefiting from their experience.

The following morning dawned into a beautiful day, full of clean, dry, fresh air, and crystal running water in the sink. We were grateful for every drop. My mother and her cousin were eager to return to the woods in search of additional mushrooms. I hurried to join them.

Building upon yesterday's circle, our conversation delved deeper. My mother and her cousin renewed their familial connection. Their talk again circled to blissful days of youth, then moved on, touching sensitive spots—pain.

After their youthful years of bathing in sunshine, a dark cloud shadowed the world. Hitler came into power. His gas chambers swallowed almost all of our family, and most of their friends. My mother and her cousin survived.

These women lived to tell their tales and share their legacy with me. I was the next generation. And as we examined mushroom after mushroom, picking some here and there, they were passing on their knowledge, giving me my inheritance. I stood with open arms, ears and heart. This mushroom legacy would not disappear into smoke, but be passed along, shared. Our circle had reached further back in time, touched earlier generations, and I was handed my heritage as a female of the Fischmann clan.

It was fitting that my mother, the eldest, would be the first to break our circle. She and my father headed off to Canada, to visit my father's only surviving relation. When I later took my mother's cousin to the airport we drove through a powerful thunderstorm. The dark, gloomy, foreboding sky sent buckets of water down to earth. And then, out of this tempest, a brilliant double rainbow was born.

The rainbow illuminated the sky, a radiant arch shining in darkness. It was the largest I'd ever seen, reaching from one side of the road to the other, circling high above our heads. We traveled straight into the rainbow for many miles, all the way to the airport. I couldn't have imagined a more fitting way to bring our weekend full circle.

On the way home I mused about this visit with my female relations. I had many treasures from our walks in the woods. The dried mushrooms were sitting in my larder, waiting to cast their spell in future generations of soup. Other treasures are preserved deep inside me. They are gifts from the grandmothers—my inheritance, my legacy as a woman.

I was initiated into a circle of women, a circle seeped in wise woman traditions, a knowledge handed down through centuries, from one person to another. This knowledge is born of the natural world, encircled by love, rooted in the earth. It's a way of knowing that incorporates all the senses, the parts as well as the whole. Healing the Feminine involves connecting with our earth and resurrecting these women's ways of knowing.

Hearing

The body is the house of our being. It houses the mind, the soul, the psyche, the spirit. We depend on our bodies for every aspect of our lives, and they serve us well.

Woman's Voice lives inside the body and speaks a body language. Her voice is a sensual voice. She's the voice of hunches, senses, feelings, and intuition.

Because we value mind over body, we tend to disregard our body's messages, tune them out, and talk about feelings in a dissociated way. Looking to clarify feelings, shed light on them, and understand them, we seem to view feelings as mental processes that are like alien beings, floating around somewhere in the psyche, not connected with the body. We've forgotten that feelings are communications. They are messages from our bodies.

Our bodies speak a somatic, metaphorical language—the language of feelings. But as our society emphasizes the masculine language of logical, rational, verbal thought, we're not facile at speaking this other language. Reclaiming Woman's Voice involves connecting with our bodies and tuning into their language. This involves another kind of hearing.

Hearing our body's messages begins with locating feelings, recognizing where we feel what we feel. It involves becoming aware of the where, focusing on where a feeling is located, and what it's like when it's there. David Grove lectures on this process of translating a feeling into its metaphorical equivalent—unfolding the embedded symbol. He emphasizes the importance of pinpointing the location of a feeling by asking "where" questions until a feeling's location is clearly identified. Once this physical location is found, he suggests asking questions such as: "Does it have a shape? ... a size? ... a color? ... a taste? ... a smell? ... a texture? ... or movement?" As these questions gather information from each of our known senses, they serve to translate a nebulous idea such as "I'm nervous, uptight" into more concrete, symbolic, somatic experiences such as: "I have knots all over my body, especially in my back," or "my shoulder muscles have coils in them."

As feelings speak a body language, it can be difficult, even impossible, finding words to describe some of them. These feelings may require another outlet for expression—another form for communication. Creative activities provide such a form because they are more concrete, symbolic, and metaphorical. Painting, sculpting, drawing, writing a poem, playing a musical instrument, and dancing offer ways of expressing feelings. They give feelings a form.

Once the feeling has a form it is easier to hear its message. It is possible to ask questions about what it wants to have happen, or what it wants to do. In this way we can hear what our body is trying to tell us. If it's hungry, it may want some food, and a particular kind of hunger might want a special food. A tired body may want to rest, or take a hot bath. And a tense body with "knots" may want a massage, while one with "coils" might ask to stretch.

When people are disconnected from their bodies they can't hear answers to these questions. They don't know how to read their body's signals, listen to their senses, and hear what their body is trying to tell them. They're dis-sociated from the information.

Reclaiming the lost part of our selves entails shifting the way we relate to our bodies. Instead of battling our bodies, trying to control them, we need to connect with them, appreciate them, and get acquainted with them. This involves developing a nurturing and caring relationship with our bodies. And while we all have issues with our bodies, women are additionally encumbered by society's attitude toward their female form which has been the object of suppression and oppression.

Many women aren't fully present in their bodies. They're battling with their embodiment of the feminine, pushing themselves out of their bodies, disowning this aspect of their selves. Some exist in a part of their bodies or float outside. Others live in their heads. Very few women are firmly rooted in their bodies.

One woman, "Emma," poignantly described this experience. She exists in her head. As she put it: "It's all in my head ... not in my body ... My head's doing everything ... My feet can move when I'm walking ... They do ... I don't ... like a head walking down the street, no body." In response to my question, Emma located herself in the area from above her eyes to the top of her head, and said that she is "a head with eyes, but a whole person in there," pointing at her forehead to identify the location of "there." Continuing to describe her experience, she said: "I live up here ... there is a downstairs, but I never go there."

When women stop battling their bodies they can start trusting their feelings and begin loving their selves. One aspect of this battle revolves around food. Thanks to society's emphasis on a slender body, many women are afraid of food. And yet food nourishes and heals us. It is our body's ally, not our enemy.

I encourage women to throw away all the diet books. Apart from the fact that they don't work, diets are quick-fix prescriptions designed to sell books— feed our country's conspicuous consumption, often at the expense of malnourishing ourselves. While our bodies are similar and require comparable forms of nourishment, my body's particular chemistry is different from yours. The best expert to consult is your own body. For those who do want to read, I recommend books that teach principles of good nutrition, such as Jane Brody's *Good Food Book* and *The New Laurel's Kitchen* by Laurel Robertson, Carol Flinders, and Brian Ruppenthal. After familiarizing yourself with the contents of books like these, put them on the reference shelf. Listen to your own body and learn how to nourish it.

While food provides nutrients essential to our physical well-being, eating is also a pleasurable experience that nourishes our psyches, our souls, and our spirit. When we savor the tart flavor of an apple or the sweet taste of a succulent fig, we are enriching many parts of our being. Considering that women are generally responsible for preparing food, it is time we also felt entitled to enjoy the satisfying sensuous aspects of food.

As our bodies aren't built for sedentary life, physical activity is another way of nurturing our bodies. Exercise nourishes the body by toning muscles, revitalizing the cardiovascular system, and getting our juices flowing. Varying the kind of exercise helps address all body functions. While aerobic activity is good for the heart, yoga stretches muscles, builds strength and flexibility. Exercise clears cobwebs out of the brain, washes soot from in front of the eyes. It cleanses the whole system, including the emotions, leaving an inner shine and outer glow.

Physical activity helps us root inside our bodies and tap into their messages. As every body is different, we each need to become familiar with our own, discover the activities we enjoy. Some people begin connecting with their bodies by playing sports such as baseball, tennis, or golf. Others enjoy more individual activities such as swimming, walking, or skiing. We learn to take care of our bodies by focusing inside, listening to feelings, noticing where we feel what we feel, and what that feeling is like when its there. By listening to our bodies and hearing what they want, we learn how to answer their requests.

Sexuality is an important, and potentially most pleasurable, physical experience. It is an opportunity to express our sensual selves in our most intimate, loving relationships. And as sensuality has been downplayed in our climax oriented culture, we are missing out on this important dimension of sexuality.

I've already discussed the fact that many women report gaining little pleasure from their sexual activities. They yearn for the touch, the embrace, the sensual experience, and wish it didn't *always* have to lead to "that." Sex therapists recognize this issue, and help clients develop the sensual side of their selves.

Couples encountering sexual difficulties such as impotence, frigidity, or premature ejaculation are usually encouraged to temporarily abstain from sexual intercourse. Coitus is prohibited and neither spouse is permitted to reach orgasm. Their sex therapist encourages them to focus on giving and receiving pleasure, rather than achieving a response, orgasm. They are encouraged to touch and caress each other, pay attention to their body's feelings in specific areas, and find out what gives them pleasure. As this process helps them tune into their sensuality, they start hearing Woman's Voice.

Woman's Voice is a sensual voice. She enjoys moving her body, tasting food, looking at beautiful scenes, smelling flowers. She wants to feel. She wants to touch and be touched. But while she enjoys expressing our innermost selves, her natural voice is often camouflaged and contained—kept hidden under perfume, behind make-up, and inside cellophane wrapping.

Healing the feminine involves taking possession of our bodies and avoiding being victimized by manufacturer's and advertiser's packaging of the feminine. Instead of blindly following fashion trends, we can listen to our own bodies, hear what looks and feels "good," what our bodies want to wear. It is important for each woman to experiment by listening to her bodily sensa-

tions—seeing what suits her physique and feeling
what pleases her aesthetic tastes. And while I person-
ally prefer wearing comfortable, attractive clothes
made of natural fibers such as cotton and silk, what
pleases my body may not please yours. We're not made
on assembly lines.

In talking about "feeling good," I'm not proposing
that we become purely narcissistic, pleasure seeking
creatures, but that we hear our body's messages and
use the information in making decisions for ourselves.
We can make choices that don't compromise our health
and well-being. For example, underwear made of syn-
thetic materials may look sexy or pretty, but as the
material doesn't "breathe," it creates an environment
in which yeast and other vaginal infections flourish.
Listening to our bodies helps avoid medication merry-
go-rounds.

When opting for health, our choices can be flexible. If our feet feel uncomfortable in small shoes or
high heels, they are trying to tell us about a problem,
and disregarding their messages can result in bunions,
corns, and shortened tendons. But we don't always
have to wear comfortable, sensible shoes. What we
wear on our feet may change from day to day, and hour
to hour, depending on the circumstances, and our
mood. As long as we continue listening to our bodies,
we'll know how to take care of ourselves.

Menstruation is a good time to listen to our bodies.
Every menstruating woman is given a monthly opportunity to pay particular attention to hearing Woman's
Voice. Starting with an array of premenstrual messages, Her voice gathers strength, increases in inten-

sity, and clamors to be heard. By unplugging Her flow we are better able to hear Her—sense our inner essence, communicate with our bodies' processes, and live in tune with our cycles.

Menstruation is often associated with a sense of tiredness. Our bodies ask us to slow down, take it easy, and get some rest. Though we tend to live hectic demanding lives, it is possible to hear our bodies' messages and find a way of answering their requests. We can try to stay in bed a little longer. Then, instead of taking a high energy run, we could go on a slow contemplative walk, or spend some time puttering in the garden. And if our life's situation precludes the possibility of an afternoon nap, we could still close the door, turn off the phone, and sit quietly by ourselves for "just a little while." We are entitled to some time for ourselves.

By taking time off from external demands, we can pay more attention to inner messages. Menstration is a time to withdraw from service to others, travel inside ourselves, and listen to Woman's Voice. Writing down dreams, painting, playing music, and free associating on paper offer ways of hearing Her messages. By hearing Her voice, we connect with ourselves.

Most women keep track of the day they start menstrating, and some of us also make note of the day we ovulate. But why limit our attention to these two special days? We can watch our energy changes throughout the month by jotting down physical, emotional, and spiritual feelings on the calendar. And as woman's body cycles with the moon, it's also interesting to watch the relationship between one's own cycle and phases of the moon. Writing down dreams, painting, playing music, and free associating on paper offer ways of hearing Her messages. By hearing Her voice, we connect with ourselves.

During menopause we move into a different aspect of the feminine. We leave our child–rearing years behind, and move on to the next phase of our lives. Our monthly cycles become erratic, wane, then disappear. Hot flashes and other changes are signs of transition and transformation; to be listened to and honored, not numbered and silenced.

While the potential turbulence of menopause is less predictable than an approximately 28-day cycle, we can flow with these inner tides and use them to connect more deeply with ourselves. The turmoil that may characterize this rite of passage gradually evolves into a calm, settled, rooted feeling. We become wise women, and it's time to pass on our wisdom, serve as models and teachers, helping girls and younger women cherish their feminine selves. In my opinion, our gray hair and wrinkles shouldn't be hidden; they're well earned and demand respect.

Healing the feminine involves valuing the female body—delighting in Her roundness, Her softness, Her cycles, Her smells, Her blood.

We embrace the feminine by celebrating our cycles, dancing to inner rhythms, expressing our sensuous sexuality, and flowing into the earth. When we tune into Her rhythms and flow with our tides, we feel good about our selves.

Developing a relationship with our bodies isn't a one way street. Our bodies give back—giving pleasure to our selves. Woman's Voice is a loving voice. We rejoice in hearing Her.

Going Natural

Woman's Voice isn't bad or evil. She is a good part of our selves. There's no need to hide her, fight her, or control her. We can trust our inner nature, and start becoming ourselves.

I remember being little, and sitting on my mother's knee while she fixed my thick, naturally curly hair. She twirled one of the many curls on my forehead, repeating a rhyme:

> There was a little girl
> Who had a little curl
> Right in the middle of her forehead
> And when she was good
> She was very very good
> And when she was bad
> She was horrid.

This rhyme initiated a struggle to tame my horrid, unruly nature—my hair.

My hair always did its thing. It curled. Not wavy, soft, sinuous curls that could easily be invited to wind their way down my back, but strong, frizzy curls going out in every direction.

My early memories of haircuts are of disappointment and tears. I recall entrusting myself into the care of an adult wielding large scissors, expecting to be re-

created, turn into a beautiful princess, Cinderella.
When the process came to an end, I looked in the mirror
and found a large, practically hairless, head staring
back at me. The trusted adult had attempted to tame
my hair by cutting off my unruly locks.

I shed many tears as this cycle repeated. Each
time I went to the "beauty" parlor hoping this time
would be different, only to have the same end result.
The hairdressers attacked my curls with a vengeance,
determined to control them, make them manageable,
keep them in their place. I cried over my lost hair, my
lost dream of Rapunzel.

During adolescence I took charge of managing my
hair. The fashionable pageboy became a personal necessity. After conducting a series of experiments, I discovered the formula for conquering the curls, forcing
them to obey my wishes and conform to this style.

While my hair was wet, I meticulously wound
clumps of hair around large rollers. Each roller was
systematically pinned around my head, until every
stubborn, unruly lock of hair was dutifully rolled into
place. Then came the lengthy, arduous task of sitting
under the hair drier for at least an hour, making sure
my thick hair would dry. The next part of the formula
involved sleeping with my hair still ensconced in rollers, a feat in and of itself, but not a restful one. The
following morning I unrolled my hair and proudly
marched off to school, flaunting my pageboy like a red
badge of courage.

Although I disliked the coarse dry texture of my
hair, it had one advantage. My hair only required a
weekly washing, which limited my hair drying ritual to
a once-a-week performance. Between these ceremonies

my hair held its shape, behaved itself, as long as I guarded against potential sabotage. Wherever I went, whatever I did, I had to protect my hair from the elements, keep it under wrap—for nature's touch immediately awakened its inclination to curl and frizz.

Styles changed and I eyed the new, shorter fashion. Once again I was seduced into visiting the hairdresser, allowing my locks to be shorn, donning the shorter style. My new look necessitated a different approach to hair management. This time I rolled some of my hair on smaller rollers, and then used a variety of clips, pins, and a piece of scotch tape to hold the rest in place during the drying process—successfully taming willful curls into gentle waves.

When the '60s brought the hippie look, it was time to let my hair grow, make it look straight. I retrieved the large rollers from their resting place, and resumed my experiments. And while I managed to mold my hair into the required shape, it was again at the expense of a good night's sleep. Finally, during my first year of graduate school, I heard about a place where one could go to get one's hair straightened. As I thought this could be the answer to my dreams, off I trotted into Harlem.

A series of chemicals were lavished on my hair, each with its unique olfactory experience, and accompanying procedure. Many hours later I emerged with hair that actually looked straight, straight as a board. Nevertheless, when I next washed my hair those errant curls readily returned, springing to life the moment they were touched by water—revived. In order to ensure that they behaved themselves, did what they were told, I needed to continue following the current hair rolling ritual. I resigned myself to a lifetime of behavior modification programs.

My experiments continued. I next discovered the art of wrapping hair. The lesson cost a pretty penny, and I came out of the beauty parlor with long, gloriously straight hair. However, I was never able to master the intricacies of this fine art. After practicing the procedure in the privacy of my bathroom, I emerged from these labors with enlarged biceps, deflated ego, and plentiful curls.

When I later began working in a psychiatric hospital, I learned something else about the rhyme of the little girl with the little curl. It was used in making the diagnosis of "hysterical personality," a diagnosis generally reserved for women and one that had derogatory implications. This diagnosis was further differentiated into "good hysteric" and "bad hysteric," depending on the level of psychosexual development. I had the markings of a good hysteric, but knew that under all that tamed hair was an unruly curl waiting to be discovered, even if she was horrid.

One day I noticed that one of the teachers had a new hair style. She was wearing an afro, and I became intrigued with the idea of letting my hair "go natural." Each time I passed her in a hallway I stared at her, wondering if my hair would take to such a style. Did it have that kind of curl? After years of setting, wrapping, and straightening, I didn't know my hair. I was unsure whether it frizzed, or whether it curled, and if it curled, how much of a curl was there. Whenever I had a chance I plied her with questions, intrigued with the possibility of being able to forgo hair conditioning treatments, and become familiar with my hair, my nature.

I became obsessed with hair, deliberating over the pros and cons of getting my hair cut. Having been burned so often before, I was wary of hairdressers, distrusted their scissors. I was proud of my long, flowing tresses, and hadn't forgotten earlier disasters, disappointments, tears. I discussed my dilemma with a friend, and discovered that she too was hankering for a change, contemplating a visit to the beauty parlor. We both wanted something to happen, to change, shift.

Buttressed by her support, I finally found the courage to have my hair cut. She decided to get hers cut locally, and I made my appointment with the person who had cut the teacher's hair. We agreed to meet after our respective appointments.

The beauty parlor reverberated with loud raucous music which didn't help settle my nerves. After changing my clothes and getting my hair washed, I eventually found my way into the hair stylist's chair. He listened to my long detailed description of what I was trying to do, then, apparently oblivious to my apprehension, proceeded to chop away at my hair, seeming to enjoy relieving me of the cherished long tresses which soon littered the floor. In terror, I pleaded with him not to cut too much off. My eyes stayed glued to the mirror, riveted, watching his every move.

When he finally finished, we surveyed his work. I stared at the strange image in the mirror. Was this me? Whoever she was, she didn't look bad. However, I wondered if she had enough curls. For the first time in my life I wanted more curls. He reassured me that my curls would readily recover from their years of suppression. They would return to their natural state.

When I arrived on my friend's doorstep she barely

recognized me. My straight long hair was nowhere to be seen. Instead, my face was surrounded by a mass of hair. I had an afro. She too looked different, changed. We kept staring at each other, at our selves, adjusting to the new images.

The next day, and for some time thereafter, my colleagues and friends had difficulty recognizing me. Everyone marveled at the transformation. I looked totally different. Many commented on my curly hair, wondered about it, asked if I'd had a perm. They were astonished to learn that this was the real me, *my* hair. The transformation was so complete that one psychiatrist continued to call me by another name for almost a year—the name of the woman whose afro I'd copied.

My new hair style occasioned a period of self discovery. I'd never known my hair, for I'd been busy struggling with it, forcing it to conform to a shape or style. Now I enjoyed watching it, playing with it, getting to know it. I'd always thought of myself as having frizzy hair, and gleefully relished the discovery that I had curls as well as frizz. I stopped trying to be like everyone else, began exploring me, the curly headed me.

For a number of years I wore variations of the afro theme, savoring my curls, enjoying new freedoms. I could go out in the rain, play a game of tennis, or dance, without worrying that my hair would revert to its natural curly state. And what a relief to no longer roll, wrap, and set my hair, sit for hours under the hair drier, and sleep on all those contraptions. I was free to be me.

Many years later I married, for the second time. After looking through picture albums, seeing me with long hair, my husband wanted me to try letting my hair grow. As I was eager to please my newfound mate, I dutifully did as he wished. And as my hair grew longer, reclaiming an unruly look, I regressed back to old patterns, resuming rolling, setting, and reshaping the thick curly locks.

After a few years struggling with my hair, I finally grew tired of the process. I spoke with my husband about cutting it, simplifying my life, reclaiming a more natural style. He was sympathetic to the time consuming aspect of my various hair rituals, and supported my decision to get a haircut.

It was with great relief that I, once again, cut my hair and let it go natural.

I enjoyed rediscovering the exhilaration of feeling free and unencumbered, the sensuous pleasures of swimming without a bathing cap, my hair rippling in the waves as the water gently massaged my scalp, and the ecstasy of taking a walk on a windy fall day, feeling the power of the wind rushing through my hair. I felt closer to nature. Nevertheless, there was one drawback. Maintaining my hair style necessitated regular visits to the hairdresser.

The hairdressers seemed determined to tame my thick, unruly hair. They attacked with their scissors, closely cropping all around my head, forcing the curls into a civilized shape. When I asked them to leave it longer, merely shape it a little, they either told me that there was no other alternative with hair such as mine or nodded, as if in acquiescence to my request, and then proceeded to put the same short style back on my head.

In desperation, I decided that the only alternative was to temporarily avoid all hairdressers. I would let my hair grow, and keep it natural. The way to discover the true nature of my hair was to give it free reign and watch what happened.

As my hair began to grow, those closest to me, my parents, husband and children, began asking when I was going to cut my hair. When I told them my plan, they immediately declared that it had gone too far. According to them, my hair stuck out, looked wild, unkempt, and unruly. Another skeptic commented that it was unbecoming for "such a petite little lady" to have a large amount of bushy hair.

Despite all the comments, I persisted in learning about my hair. I was determined to discover my me, my nature. And while I knew that I would eventually cut my hair, I would no longer attempt to tame my unruly locks. They would be free to express their nature. I would be fully my self.

The curl in the middle of my forehead is no longer little and neither am I. We're not very very good. We're not horrid. We're *me*.

Centering

Sometimes we "just know" something and if someone asks how we know what we know, we may not have an objective reason for our knowledge. We call this knowing in-tuition, inner seeing, a knowing that comes from within. This way of knowing is one that uses senses, including ones we may not know we have. It is "a woman's way of knowing."

Woman's way of knowing seems to emanate from the pit of the stomach, from our center. As we've been cut off from this central place inside ourselves, healing the feminine involves developing a different relationship with our bellies. When we move into this inner place of balance, we tap our source of creative energy.

The current epidemic of eating disorders is a symptom of our society's imbalance, and personal off-centeredness. As we've been battling our bellies, our centers are starved, malnourished, and crying out for attention. We need to welcome their messages and hear what they're trying to tell us, but after years of dissociating ourselves from our centers this isn't as simple as it sounds.

Over the past few years I've been connecting with my belly and learning to hear its messages. It's been a complicated, exciting process, involving many aspects of my life, including the food I eat. My eating patterns shifted as I moved inside my body and felt its messages.

After a short battle with my bulge during adolescence, I managed to stay slender for the next twenty years. During this time I closely monitored my weight by eating meat and avoiding starch. This eating pattern changed when the pressures of feeding a large family gave birth to an interest in healthy food. And while I still tried to avoid gaining weight, my primary concern was my family's health and well-being.

Once I started down the road toward healthful eating, one thing led to another and I became a vegetarian. As my family wasn't interested in taking this giant step, I continued cooking meat and fish for them. My switch to vegetarianism was primarily motivated by philosophical and nutritional concerns, but I also sensed some other purpose was being served. I was making an internal shift that involved defining myself, differentiating between my desires and my family's. It was a way of making sure I wasn't consumed by my husband and children, swallowed up by their never ending wants and desires.

In becoming a vegetarian I'd gone from one extreme to another, from a diet of primarily meat to one of only vegetables. At first I felt well, lost some weight, and moved closer to my earlier form. But then my scale sent other messages. It started inching up, and my alarm increased along with the numbers. As I knew my body was trying to tell me something, I wanted to listen to it, understand its messages.

My body kept sending messages that something was wrong. As I was feeling ravenous in the afternoon and tending to overeat, I first analyzed my binges, asking whether I was feeling empty, depleted, or unfulfilled. And while I unearthed useful and interesting feelings, these discoveries didn't explain a phase of drinking coffee, an unhealthy substance that hadn't interested me for over thirty years, or a period of craving chocolate, another novel experience.

In trying to remedy my symptoms, but not knowing how to hear my body's signals, I was like a would-be swimmer who doesn't trust the body to float. I was flailing my arms, grabbing hold of one thing then the next. My husband teased me about my periodic kicks, for one year I'd eat plenty of yogurt then the next none at all. I knew my afternoon raids on the granola jar weren't "just lapses in will power." Something was out of balance, and I didn't know what.

After seven years of strict vegetarianism, I wondered if I was eating enough protein and decided to bend my rules, become more flexible, and start eating fish. This experiment was well underway when my husband and I went on vacation to the Pacific Northwest. We spent some time together, some apart, and I had one particularly glorious morning of walking, hiking, being by myself and connecting with my body while my husband went on a salmon hunting expedition. As my husband's exhilarating day netted a number of salmon, the chef prepared one for our supper.

My husband raved about the salmon and I initially agreed with him. But in the middle of eating the salmon, I suddenly didn't want any more. My body was clearly telling me it wanted veggies, lots and lots of them. At the risk of insulting my husband, I listened to my body and stopped eating the salmon.

After this experience I continued trusting my senses. Instead of standing outside my body and looking in, I tried listening from inside. This shift in perspective made all the difference. When I centered *inside* my stomach, I realized that I was hungry in the morning. Ever since my first adolescent diet I had trained myself not to hear my morning hunger. No wonder I was starving in the afternoon!

In retrospect, I'd been living outside my belly, watching, interpreting, and looking for explanations of my particular behavior in the unending supply of nutrition books and dietary fads. Each dietary approach made sense, but my problem hadn't been with yogurt or protein. I hadn't been centering, sensing, listening from inside my belly.

While my dietary flip-flops gave the impression that I was jumping from one extreme to the next, I was gradually inching into my center. I wasn't following a "diet," but trusting my feelings and searching to hear my body's messages. My body's response to each successive change was information helping me move towards the center. My final leap in was an act of faith. Breakfast has become my favorite meal—a pleasurable way to start every day.

In my experience, a woman's psychological and physical malnourishment is centered in the belly area, and many women describe feeling like they have a hole in their stomach. Though the psychoanalysts think of a woman's hole as referring to her vagina, I've found that women are usually referring to their bellies. Some women have big black empty holes; others have bottomless pits. And while they look for something to fill it, usually nothing can. But when they begin centering, something else happens with their "hole."

As women turn inward, center inside the self, and become grounded there, they report feeling more whole. They no longer feel fragmented, disconnected, but a whole self ready to express their self. The process of centering helps their "hole" gradually evolve into a "w-hole."

Centering involves tuning into the self, physically and emotionally. It entails finding the inner place of balance where information about ourselves, and also other people, comes together. When we center ourselves inside this space it becomes our central place for connection and interconnection. Hearing our own wants, wishes and desires, gives us the opportunity to nourish our centers. And as this place is no longer blocked off from the rest of ourselves, we're not limited to only taking in. We can also express our selves—flow from within.

As we become more centered, we discover how to nurture our selves. We learn to differentiate between different forms of hunger, and the difference between nourishing our bodies and feeding our centers. While we may nourish our bodies with wholesome food, exercise, rest and massage, we fill our centers by fulfilling our selves, being fully ourselves, flowing from our bellies.

Many small acts go into centering. It's not something that is done once and for all. But once a woman starts finding her center, and living within this inner space, it's easier to get back there each time she's blown off course. She can use it to anchor herself—her place of inner mooring.

Many women say it is easier to stay centered when they are by themselves. They have more difficulty being themselves, hearing themselves, being present in themselves when they're with other people. This is especially the case when they're with people they care deeply about—their children, husband, boyfriend, lover, parents. As long as they're not involved with other people they can hear their own voice, feel solid, confident, and secure. This changes the minute someone special enters their picture. Then they become confused about what they want, and stop being able to hear themselves. They get distracted by the external voices, pulled outside. It's much easier to feel centered while alone or when not in a relationship with a valued person.

Knowing how to center doesn't mean one never feels off-center. I also have difficulty staying centered when I'm around other people. My tendency is to join with them, become centered outside of myself. The trick is to learn how to stay centered while with other people, to be able to join with them, care about them, feel for them, and not to lose the sense of centeredness when also connected with someone else. This is a more difficult process—one that may sometimes seem impossible, but is, nonetheless, worth aiming to achieve—to be centered *and* connected.

I spent many years of my life focused outside my self. While I considered myself to be in touch with my feelings, especially after years of psychotherapy, I focused on other people. I wasn't centered in myself.

A number of vehicles have helped me move into myself, and one of them is yoga. After taking yoga for a couple of years I knew that I always left class feeling relaxed, refreshed, renewed. Then came one particularly hectic, unsettling, unsatisfactory day. Nothing had gone right. By the time I arrived at my yoga class I was tired, frazzled, cranky, and irritable. My nerves were frayed.

The class began and I proceeded to stretch and breathe. The tension began releasing, and the day's events receded into the background. I left class feeling rejuvenated and centered.

Reflecting on this experience I realized that yoga had been teaching me how to still my self and settle into myself. I'd learned how to use my breath to move into the space inside my self. Nevertheless, there were too many occasions when I wasn't centered. I seemingly knew how to get centered, but didn't know how to stay centered.

It has taken me quite a while to learn about remaining centered when buffeted by people, crises, and unexpected turns of events. I've learned to create spaces within which to regroup myself, pull my self back to center. If possible, I try to take a walk, ground my self. However, there isn't enough time in the day to take a walk each time I want to create space for myself. As it only takes a few seconds to breathe, I can always use my breath to move into my inner space, remain there momentarily, and connect with my center. Whenever I do this throughout the day I find that I'm better equipped to enter whatever is happening while staying inside my center, my sense of purposeful direction.

While many people don't know how to begin locating "their center," they can learn belly breathing. Once they let go of holding their stomachs in and constricting their breath, they can learn a modified form of meditation. This involves sitting quietly and paying attention to their breath, watching the breath as it goes in and out of their stomach. After they've practiced this simple technique for a while, they inadvertently learn to use their breath to take them into their center, and breathe life into the center of their selves. And as the breath nourishes their center, they can attend to internal messages by listening and hearing from here.

Centering is empowering, for a woman's creative center, her source, is in her belly. When a woman sends her roots into this center she taps the source of her energy, her power, her passion. She becomes powerful. Her power comes from within, from her inner nature, the feminine. It isn't power over, but power to, for and with.

The issue of power usually brings up all sorts of associations. We generally think of power hierarchically, as power over—people and nations jockeying to be the one on top, not to be the underdog. The power I'm talking about is another kind of power. Empowerment moves horizontally, not vertically. Empowerment is power to.

Many women share a common dilemma. While they're not comfortable with the hierarchical form of power, they haven't learned another way of expressing themselves. One woman recently put it this way. She was struggling to handle a situation and saw herself as having one of two options. She could either "lie down, like a doormat and let them walk all over me" . . . or . . . "start yelling at them . . . fight." Becoming centered offers a third option—that of standing firmly in one's ground, being solidly there, speaking from there.

After being focused outside themselves for many years some women go through a period of inner absorption and learning to say "No" to other people. And while they may worry about becoming "too self-ish," this is a phase of supporting themselves and establishing inner roots. Once they feel firmly planted inside their selves, more centered, these women develop a relaxed way of ensuring they don't compromise themselves.

Centering is living inside polarities. A woman who is "centered" is planted in her body, rooted in the soil of her self. And while she lives in her center, deriving strength and power from here, she also connects with other people, cares about them, and gives to them. Her caring for others is balanced by an investment in her self.

Integrating

Mind *and* Body

Mind and body aren't separate entities. While they have distinct functions, they work in unison, in tandem. Their complicated communication network is responsible for keeping us alive and well.

Even though mind and body are interdependent, many people think that the neck separates their mind from their body. These people may see their body as having a mind of its own, especially when it seemingly does things they wish it didn't do. They think with their heads, and try to use their minds to control their bodies. These attempts to rule the body are usually doomed to failure, for the body generally does as it's told. It believes everything it hears.

The body responds to whatever information is transmitted to it. If you are frightened, threatened, or anxious, your body reacts accordingly by preparing for danger—discharging adrenalin and readying muscles for action. It doesn't differentiate between an imagined danger and a real one.

When you are afraid, you think about your fear, about what may happen, possibly also visualizing the gory details. If you are afraid to fly you might imagine the plane crashing, an engine failing, or a hijacking. The minute you begin thinking this way your body starts preparing for danger. It can't tell the difference between an imaginary plane crash and a real one.

Panic and stress disorders owe their peculiarities to this complementary relationship between body and mind. The body is doing what it's told to do—getting ready for action. But it has been sent the wrong information. Anxious people imagine dangers, and people who are "under stress" contend with psychological threat. While neither involves any real physical danger, the body readies itself to act, to physically protect itself. As there is nothing the body is required to do, this physiological state of arousal has no way of dissipating. If this condition continues, it produces symptoms such as increased cholesterol, high blood pressure, and stomach problems.

My husband had a digestive disorder for many years. He has a high pressure job and is constantly stressed. When his stomach first began troubling him he went through the usual battery of gastrointestinal tests. As these diagnostic procedures were inconclusive, he tried a variety of medications, and began supporting the antacid industry. In addition, he became suspicious of certain foods and eliminated them from his diet.

My husband didn't realize that his body was constantly preparing for battle. Everything else, including digesting food, was put on hold. This condition became chronic as it continued year after year. His complaints of bloating, heartburn, and other discomfort increased. Finally, in desperation, he began doing things to alleviate his stress. He is now feeling much better, and can sometimes eat food that is more difficult to digest, the things that were causing him the most distress. When he's relaxed, unpressured by work, his body can attend to food.

As today's stresses are primarily psychological, our bodies are prone to develop stress related symptoms. These symptoms are messages from the body, warnings that something is out of balance. While it is preferable to make adjustments that correct the imbalance by eliminating the source of the problem, it is possible to counteract some of the ravages of stress. This can be done by taking steps to regularly reduce the level of physiological arousal. Exercise is one way to do this, for it puts the body to work, thereby releasing muscular tension. Relaxation techniques are another way to let go of stress.

Many people, especially those with anxiety problems, benefit from learning how to relax. I often teach clients my favorite relaxation technique, a modified version of meditation. They learn to take a few slow deep breaths, and to focus on releasing tension with each out breath, letting go of tension each time they breathe. A few long deep breaths spaced throughout each day calms frazzled nerves. It can help deal with tension while sitting in a traffic jam, or waiting on a supermarket line.

Progressive muscle relaxation is also useful. This technique involves focusing on a body area, releasing tension, then moving on to the next location. Tensing a muscle before relaxing it helps some people differentiate between the two conditions. My clients learn to travel from one end of the body to the other, consciously focusing on specific muscle groups, systematically letting go of tension in every part of the body. While this technique can be used any time of the day, it is also helpful for someone having trouble falling asleep. Insomniacs prepare for sleep by lying in bed and focusing on releasing tension from every part of the body.

The complementary relationship between mind and body has its advantages. There is power in positive thinking. And while I don't expect people to be able to flip a switch which turns negative thoughts into positive ones, I do teach people about the power of the mind. The mind can be used to influence the body, not by battling against it or trying to control it, but by working with it. Some stress management techniques are based on this principle, using soothing sounds and pleasant imagery to promote physical relaxation.

Mental imagery can promote healing and help maintain the tone of immobilized muscles. I told my mother about this technique when she broke her ankle a number of years ago. She practiced it religiously, devoting some time every day to a scenario where she imagined her bones mending, pictured it in her mind's eye. In addition, she mentally exercised all her stationary muscles. She made a rapid, complete recovery, which is quite an accomplishment for a woman her age. Similar techniques have also been used with cancer patients who imagine their "killer" T cells attacking cancerous growths.

I used mental imagery with a client, "Pam," who started having migraines. She began one of her sessions telling me about her recent headaches. And while she might otherwise have taken a pill, she was pregnant and avoiding medication. Not only was she suffering, enduring throbbing pain, but her income was being affected. Whenever the headache struck she became incapacitated. She was frequently leaving work, running home to rest, and waiting for it to disappear.

I had learned about migraines in a behavioral medicine course. They are often associated with cold hands and cold feet. One of the medications used to alleviate migraines is a vasodilator, designed to increase the flow of blood to the hands and feet, subsequently decreasing the amount in blood vessels of the brain. The person teaching the course suggested that mechanically warming the extremities while simultaneously cooling the forehead produces the same desired effect.

I shared this knowledge with Pam, including some thoughts about how she might warm her hands and feet. She could either immerse them in a bath tub filled with warm water while applying a cold compress on her forehead, or get into a warm bed with electric blanket at full blast, again putting a cold pack on her forehead. After offering these ideas I thought of another option—using mental imagery.

Migraines can be precipitated by stress, and we were probably talking about a stressful subject when Pam felt a headache beginning. Her attention immediately focused on the pain, and she was tempted to run home to the comfort of her bed. Instead, I suggested we seize the opportunity and try using imagery. She was eager to experiment.

Pam was familiar with relaxation techniques, for I had taught her how to let go of tension in her muscles and focus on her breath. So she closed her eyes, began breathing slowly and rhythmically, gradually calming her body, allowing tension to be released. When I could see she had begun to relax, I suggested that she might want to begin warming her hands and feet, while cooling her head. I encouraged her to focus on warming images—to imagine the warm rays of a bright summer sun falling on her hands and feet, bringing their warmth to her finger tips, fingers, hands, toes and feet. Not only did her headache go away, but she never had another one. She was able to use imagery whenever she felt a migraine in the offing.

Even though Pam's migraine headaches were probably induced by hormonal changes, she was able to influence them with mental imagery. Unfortunately modern medicine overlooks many similar healing resources. It doesn't deal with wellness, with the process of health, wholeness, but looks at health in increasingly minute pieces. Each specialist is highly knowledgeable about one aspect of the body, but often ignorant about the whole, the way the parts participate in the whole health of the person.

The increasing fragmentation of modern medicine unfortunately produces physicians who behave like horses wearing blinders. All they see is a small section of the universe. As they're unable to open their eyes, see the whole perspective, they're stuck looking at the horizon, believing the earth is flat.

I don't believe that health professionals can effectively treat a part of a person without paying attention to the whole. A holistic approach is one which takes into account all the various contributing factors. It addresses underlying processes of "disease" and synthesizes information into a whole picture. Fortunately, a few physicians have begun making important contributions in this area. For example, Dr. Dean Ornish's pioneering "Opening Your Heart" program has proved that severe heart disease can be reversed through lifestyle changes which include diet, stress management, meditation, and a variety of other psychological techniques.

Staying healthy is a process, a way of life. Rather than numbing the body to deal with illness, anesthetizing symptoms, I recommend you listen to your symptoms and use the available healing resources of both your body and mind. Living a healthy, whole life involves expanding horizons rather than narrowing them, seeing that the earth is round rather than flat, and recognizing that we have a body and a mind.

Your body and mind are eager to work together, harmonize, join forces. Listen to the wisdom of your body. She never lies.

Masculine *and* Feminine

I started becoming conscious of feminist issues during my late twenties. As I opened my eyes, saw what I'd never allowed myself to see, I recognized inequities between men and women. And while I was angry, I didn't blame the men in my life. They weren't responsible for women's wounds.

Looking back on those years of slow awakening, I recall struggling to articulate my concerns. And as I started being more vocal, direct, and outspoken, I became concerned that someone might accuse me of being a "castrating female." This phrase was more common back then, but is still in use today.

At the time I wasn't aware of concerns about my self—that my anger might begin to show, be perceived as castrating. I became angry about the term itself. It became the focus for my anger, something I could talk about, safely.

I recall a number of social occasions when I went on a diatribe against this phrase. While I tried not to ruffle too many feathers, I was outspoken about my distaste for these words. I complained to both men and women, patiently pointing out that while a man was expected to be assertive, an assertive woman was read-

ily labeled a "castrating bitch." Moreover, a man deni-
grating a woman was merely making sure that the
woman toes the line, stays in her place. It was acceptable for a man to act superior, put down someone of the
opposite sex. Women were not allowed to behave this
way.

The worst labels a woman could hurl at a man
were: You're "a bastard," or a "son of a bitch." These
epithets placed responsibility for the man's behavior
on the shoulders of a woman, his mother. He wasn't
held responsible. It was her fault.

After these early beginnings of growing awareness, I again closed my eyes. I was too busy connecting
with men, building relationships with them, caring for
them, to allow myself to entertain any "radical" ideas.
Moreover, I suffered from a major misunderstanding,
one that is common, even among the ranks of feminists.
I'd fallen into society's trap of identifying male with
masculine and female with feminine.

While I didn't blame men for the cultural bias
against women, I saw the issue as male and female—
males were subjugating females. This perspective was
shortsighted, for I was blind to the deeper issues. Nevertheless, when I was dating I complained about the
multitude of men who seemed unable to remain close,
were afraid of relationships, and wanted to maintain
their independence. I didn't see that these crippled
men were afflicted by the same disease. They'd been
required to denounce the feminine inside their selves.

Unaware that I was suffering from an illusion,
misconstruing the issues, I sensed that if I were to own
my anger about inequities between men and women I
might turn that anger on men, blame them, see them

as the guilty party. As I somehow knew they weren't responsible for my plight, woman's condition, I was caught in a quandary. The issue went underground.

Hidden from sight, these concerns continued to fester. They resonated with the voices in my office, waiting to resurrect in a different form. When they emerged, they had different faces, and I had different words. My clients had introduced me to the other side of their selves—the dark side, the feminine.

As I listened to the voices in my office I heard an underlying theme. Everyone was trying to live up to society's expectation of them. While men desperately struggled to live up to society's standards of "masculine" behavior, women tried equally hard to be "feminine." Yet those who were ostensibly most successful in living up to these ideals sensed that something wasn't quite right. Some were acting out their distress by having affairs, drinking, and developing eating disorders. Others reported feeling incomplete, unfulfilled, unhappy.

In trying to fulfill society's expectations, my clients had cut off important parts of their selves. While the women were unable to become themselves, the men were denying their softer, sensitive side. Everyone was struggling with something inside, battling with it, trying to get rid of it. They were dismembered from an aspect of their selves—the feminine.

Men denounce the feminine side of their nature, for they are brought up suppressing their feelings, distrusting intuition, valuing reason. And when some married men begin having affairs, they often can't understand what's happening. They come to me, wondering if they still love their wives, speculating about what to do.

One such client, "David," was a very moral man. He was a caring person, a responsible father, husband and son. Yet every now and again he was attracted to another woman, drawn to her. Each time this happened he came to see me, wondering what was going on. After a few such visits he decided to continue with therapy.

Whenever I asked about feelings, David had difficulty answering my questions. He tried to understand why he was drawn to these other women, but couldn't identify the feelings. The most he could say was that he knew he was looking for "something." As he was acting out his feelings instead of experiencing them, we began looking at his behavior, trying to read between its lines in order to understand what was happening.

David was the epitome of the rational male. He had high expectations of himself and always tried to behave in a reasonable manner. These efforts generally paid off, for he was highly regarded in the community and successful in his line of work. However, he was so busy doing the right thing that he never had much fun.

As we continued working together David was gradually able to identify a few feelings, and a pattern began to emerge. His attractions seemed to take place when he felt most devoid of feeling. The "something" he was looking for had to do with feeling.

David's attractions initially sparked some fires inside his self, and then rapidly extinguished under the cool winds of reality. They were doomed to fail and be repeated again and again. This symptom contained his lost voice. It was the voice of the feminine, the feminine inside his self.

David hadn't known where to look for his "something." He was firmly entrenched in the masculine, and had banished the feminine from inside his self. Yet he yearned for Her, kept searching for Her. And while he sensed that his "something" had to do with the feminine, he looked for Her in all the wrong places, outside himself.

Many of us have been looking for "something" outside ourselves, when "it" has been inside all along. Woman's Voice is the dis-membered voice. She is dissociated, and we've been searching, trying to find Her. As much as men squelch their feelings, they yearn to feel. And though women may push themselves out of their bodies, they yearn to live there, be rooted in the soil of their selves. We seek to re-member, possess Her—our bodies, our feelings, the feminine side of our selves.

While I believe that we need to embrace the feminine, I'm not suggesting that this be done at the expense of the masculine. Valuing the feminine, cherishing Her, does not entail supplanting the masculine. She adds to Him, balances Him. Both are necessary parts of our whole.

Many of today's "successful" women have learned to live in a masculine world. While they're comfortable with the masculine side of their selves, these women frequently worry about their femininity. They're concerned that their "strength" detracts from their attractiveness as women.

One such woman, "Joan," feels competent in her work. However, she is insecure about her more intimate relationships, particularly with men. Like some

other unmarried "successful" women, she worries
about intimidating men, scaring them away. When she
is in social situations she refrains from mentioning her
occupation or minimizes her position. She wants to be
seen as "feminine."

Joan also displaces these concerns onto her body.
While some women might envy her slender shape, she
sees her body as too thin, lacking feminine curves. She
isn't "soft" enough.

Another woman, "Wendy," describes herself as
caught between two worlds. Each world has different
expectations. In the world of work she is expected to be
assertive, confident, and sure of her self. At home she is
supposed to defer to her husband, behave "like a
woman." Wendy is so busy trying to live up to different
expectations that she is never herself.

These women are not strange or unique, for all my
clients face similar dilemmas. They feel they have to
choose. They can be either masculine or feminine, but
they can't be both.

Men are afraid that if they allow themselves to
empathize, tap into their reservoirs of feeling, they
cease being masculine. To be a man they have to be
tough, hard, and unyielding. My female clients express
the same dilemma, but in different terms. They are
concerned that men will reject them if they act self-
confident, entitled, sure of themselves. Men will no
longer be attracted to them. They wouldn't be feminine.

While there are obvious differences between men
and women, the polarization of masculine and feminine is culturally created, defined, and perpetuated. It
is an artificial, theoretical polarity, one that is useful in

describing concepts such as those in this book. However, it isn't to be identified with male and female.

Men and women are people, human beings, not artificial abstractions. The assumption that males should only be masculine and females feminine overlooks the inner richness and infinite diversity inherent in each person. It forces males to suppress the "feminine" aspects of their selves and females to do similarly with the "masculine." Masculine and feminine are both aspects of our selves, albeit in different proportions for each of us.

We've been maltreating our inner environment, nurturing a few select seeds while forcing others to lie dormant. And if those dormant seeds struggle for life and manage to survive, we've seen them as weeds and uprooted our inner beds. Only the prized seeds are encouraged to thrive.

Instead of subjugating a part of our selves, we can look to integrate the self. Nature has bequeathed Her diversity Her wholeness. Our inner environment has fertile soil in which many seeds can take root, grow, flourish and flower. And while we may wish to cultivate some special gifts, nature's diversity offers balance, wholeness. By mending the internal rifts, she helps us integrate our selves.

Integration doesn't involve merging all aspects of the self into one standard form. It grants the integrity of each contributing element, valuing the uniqueness of each. Each part offers its balancing aspect to the whole, an ever evolving, changing, multifaceted whole. With Her help we can move towards becoming whole human beings—nurture our masculine and feminine traits, nourish the inner garden. We can embrace our feminine, as well as our masculine.

Now that I no longer identify masculine and feminine with male and female, I've stopped worrying that my strength will jeopardize a man's sense of himself. True manliness doesn't depend on woman's weakness. Moreover, it can be a great relief for a man to know that he needn't be strong all the time. He can nourish the feminine aspects of himself which, paradoxically, is closer to the original intent of castration.

Studies of mythology suggest that men tried to "make women" of themselves hoping to achieve woman-like fertility, for there was yet no recognition of the male reproductive role. Various rituals were performed to achieve this goal. One of which, ceremonial castration, was a primitive attempt to turn a male body into a female form—replace dangling genitalia with a bleeding hole (Walker, 1983).

While we no longer practice such gory procedures, men continue searching for the feminine. Rather than maiming their bodies, or sowing their wild seeds elsewhere, they can allow the feminine to grow inside their selves. The feminine balances their masculine.

Some women already value the masculine side of their selves. Others can develop this strength. They can be logical and creative, rational and irrational, strong and weak, soft and hard. They can know in their stomachs as well as their heads.

The feminine has been lost to all of us. But we're coming out of the dark ages, approaching the dawn of a new awakening. She's been raising Her voice demanding to be heard. And we've begun to listen. Her presence is being felt. We will have masculine *and* feminine.

And

Our inner lives intertwine with whatever happens outside our selves. The intrapsychic is tied to the interpersonal. There are no dividing lines.

We live in a world where the masculine emphasis on separation and autonomy is valued at the expense of the more feminine orientation towards connection. Dichotomous, either/or, thinking is built into the foundation of our culture. It permeates every aspect of our lives, structuring every perception and all our relationships.

Politics is entrenched in the either/or. We used to think that either America has power, or Russia would dominate. Then came "glasnost," and after that the Gulf crisis—a power struggle with Saddam Hussein. Sometimes I feel that we behave like Don Quixote, for we chase one adversary after another, and continue believing that either we wield power over others, or "they" will see us as weak. We don't explore other forms of power because we've been trained to think in terms of power over rather than power with. Our minds are ruled by the either/or.

Either/or thinking is divisive. It maintains distinctions and separations. By forcing choice between this and that, the either/or divides energy, distracts from any possibility of mutual direction, sharing. Using an either/or puts a road block in one path, creating detours, distractions, and diverting energy into two directions rather than one. This way of thinking diffuses energy by establishing adversarial relationships.

The use of "either/or" creates a competitive framework. It suggests that both options cannot be possible. And while this may sometimes be true, often it isn't.

I remember my mother's desperate voice demanding that I eat all my dinner or forgo dessert. She used similar threats whenever she felt powerless, whenever she was trying to move me in a particular direction, get me to do something. As usual, I obeyed my mother. I finished dinner without ever considering the possibility that I was full and might wish to forgo dessert.

When I later became a parent, I found my voice echoing hers as I faced comparable situations with my children. Searching for a way of influencing their behavior, I reached into early memories, began meting out similar either/or options. I wasn't happy saying all those either/ors, but didn't know what else to do. More recently, I've been learning about the power of "and."

"Ands" establish a different kind of power. They are empowering—rising above artificial distinctions, creating potential for mutual direction. "Ands" are cumulative. They join together, sum up, add potential to potential rather than subtract or divide. All sorts of things become possible with an "and." Nothing happens when you are stuck between an "either" and an "or."

Whenever I told my son "either you get home at five o'clock *or* you'll be grounded tomorrow," we generally stayed stuck in whatever pattern had culminated in that juncture. A battle of wills ensued, all because of the "or." The "or" came between my son and I, just as it effectively separated one day from the next. He was trapped into deciding between whether he wanted to stay out late one day *or* be able to go out the next. Generally he opted for immediate gratification, managing to get home late, which precipitated the next go around. Neither of us "won."

Now that I'm older and wiser, I've considered what might have happened if I'd suggested that my son "get home at five o'clock today *and* begin planning something for tomorrow." The "and" changes the intention. It sets up a positive potential rather than a threat, empowers rather than disempowers. While I'll never know what my son would have done, I suspect that we might have been able to shift from an adversarial position toward one of mutuality.

The divisiveness of either/or thinking doesn't just apply to interpersonal relationships. Some people get stuck in an internal quagmire of choice, paralyzed by a multitude of alternatives. These people are prone to obsess. They see every step of life in terms of "eithers" and "ors." Each either/or situation opens up another, until they are lost in a maze of choice. They go round and around, seeing possibilities everywhere, creating endless lists of options. As they're torn between every "either" and "or," they never see the "and." In their struggle to make the right decision, they are unable to make any decision.

I'm not suggesting that we stop making responsible choices. It is important to be able to recognize options. However, there are many situations where the choices are irrelevant or unnecessary—determined by our tendency towards divergent thinking, rather than being inherent in the situation. Each day presents countless examples of either/or situations which can be shifted using "and." The "and" is an empowering alternative to the entrapping "either/or."

Many people believe that loving someone precludes having negative feelings towards that person. *Either* they love that person *or* they don't. This assumption often crops up in therapy when clients begin talking negatively about a parent. After complaining about something a parent did or said, they say something like: "I feel guilty saying these things about my father." They feel they must refrain from criticizing their parents. Sometimes they immediately go on to describe their parent's good qualities.

Therapists recognize that people have positive and negative feelings. Ambivalence is normal. And while we may differ in our therapeutic approach, we all generally aim to modify clients' either/or assumptions about feelings. I purposefully emphasize the "and," letting my clients know that they may well love their parents *and* be angry about something they said or did. And, I never argue with clients about guilt, for they may express their negative feelings *and* feel guilty.

In a totally different situation, one of my clients, "Marsha," had struggled with a long standing depression. After almost a year of therapy, she started feeling better and wanted to begin making changes in her life. However, she'd been so focused on other people that she'd lost touch with her self and didn't know what she wanted. As our work continued Marsha started feeling entitled to want things for herself, and then gradually began the process of defining her wants.

Marsha recently came in and announced that she wants to go to law school. After making this declaration she repeated herself, adding the word "really" to emphasize the depth of her desire. Then she began to cry, saying "I'm scared." She went on to say that she's afraid to want because she may not get what she wants. And, as she wants to go to law school, she's afraid to complete the application.

Marsha only saw one choice. She could *either* complete the application for law school *or* she could be afraid of not being accepted. As I listened to her, I heard another option, that of completing the application *and* being afraid. She didn't have to stop being afraid in order to complete the application.

Another client, "Doris," who I've mentioned before, came in for a session complaining that, as usual, she had no time for her self. She is constantly overextended, stressed and depleted. Her life is a whirlwind of activity centered around her family's needs, including taxiing her children from here and there—to sports events, medical appointments, and visits to friends. In addition to her usual stresses, we were approaching a holiday season with its added responsibilities, including visitors.

One of the visitors wanted to see a sick relative while in the area, and Doris felt obligated to take her there. Even though the visitor had made it clear she understood it might be too hectic an undertaking, Doris was having difficulty denying the request. She believed that if she said no to this request and remained at home, her children would then expect her to be available for their errands. It was as if she had a choice between becoming further taxed *either* by her visitor *or* her children. When I inquired about her children's requests for rides she commented that they are generally reasonable. Her decisions about whether or not to give a child a ride are based upon whether *or* not the request is "reasonable."

There are obviously many issues involved in this situation. One of them has to do with Doris's either/ors. She was caught in a multitude of either/ors, embedded in a matrix of no-win situations. She had not considered the possibility that she could say no to the visitor's request *and* say no to her children. In addition, she did not recognize that a request could be reasonable *and* she could say no. Our session focused on these "ands" as I encouraged Doris to consider her needs and see herself as part of the whole. The "and" empowered her, gave her another option, one where she could choose to do something for herself.

The power of "and" is apparent everywhere. In interpersonal relationships, "ands" can empower individuals while simultaneously encouraging connection. "Ands" encourage movement that recognizes potential for a whole.

Many marriages run into difficulty when they lose sight of the "and." Marriages are formed between people who are inherently different from one another. Even though there is often the glow of discovering a soul mate, a shared bond, a communality of feeling, there are always differences, for no two people are exactly alike. The fine art of building a marriage entails cherishing the differences, using them to complement one another, add to the marriage rather than detract from it. Marriages run into difficulty with this process when they get stuck in the either/or.

Some women turn to therapy when their marriages flounder. They feel depressed and don't know where else to turn. I look to recognize when the difficulty lies in the marriage itself—when it's the marriage that needs help rather than the individual who initially seeks me out.

In a typical scenario, one woman came to see me because she was depressed. As usual, I obtained a brief history. Each time I asked her a question about herself, she answered in terms of her husband. She complained about how he had changed, and attributed her difficulties to changes in their relationship.

While she and her husband used to be close, they had drifted apart from one another. They were spending very little time alone together, tending to focus all of their together time around their children. Suspecting that she and her husband needed to re-engage with each other, I began asking about activities they could do together. She parried each question by pointing out their differences, telling me that they liked different things. One area we discussed was movies.

She and her husband like going to movies. But they have dissimilar tastes. While he wants to see foreign movies, ones that make him think, she wants to be entertained. She wants to laugh, have fun, and see light movies, rather than ones with heavy social messages. Each time they try to decide upon a movie they argue about whether to see a movie he wants *or* one she would like. Rather than continue to battle, they stopped going to movies. Instead of adding to their relationship, they subtracted from their experiences together.

I suggested that she and her husband begin using the "and." Instead of avoiding movies, they could take turns. They could go together, and alternate the type of movie they would see. While they might not like the same movies, they might be surprised to discover that they enjoy themselves more than they expect. They would also be together, sharing an activity, and talking about something other than "the children."

When people begin using the "and" it shifts their perception, changing their relationship with each other as well as their selves. This one word can make a world of difference in a world of differences. It can enable connection where there is disconnection—collaboration in place of competition. Separate people can connect with one another.

The same principles apply to international relations. Countries can use their power cooperatively, their strength for a greater good. Nations can work together toward mutual goals, not by becoming subsumed in one another, but connected, joined together by "ands" that respect each other's separateness. Each nation is part of a whole, a part-nership with planet Earth. We can live in harmony with each other and within our selves.

Nature

Masculine and feminine are both present in nature. Nature is linear and circular, active and passive, predictable and unpredictable, nurturing and punitive, warm and cold. Apparent opposites balance each other, creating a whole.

In earlier times we saw ourselves as intertwined with nature—part of the whole. But as civilization became increasingly mechanized, dominated by the masculine, the feminine was relegated outside, to nature's domain. Society was identified with the masculine, and nature with the feminine.

As a result of many societal changes that have been thoroughly described by Marilyn French (1985), Carolyn Merchant (1980), and Susan Griffin (1978), nature was set up as the counterpoint of culture—the repository of the irrational, the unpredictable, the feminine. We lost our collaborative relationship with nature, and as "She" became the enemy, issues of control pervade our attitude towards nature. We now readily defoliate "mother earth" with modern versions of the Vietnam War's agent orange, renamed herbicide 2-4-D. And we battle "her" bugs outside and inside our bodies, using pesticides outside, antibiotics inside.

We've continued to move further and further apart from nature. Instead of living in a natural world, we live ensconced in a hi-tech world of megabytes and megabits. Our thinking is mechanistic, and we even think of ourselves in mechanistic terms. Feelings get "turned on" and "turned off," controlled by a switch.

Technological "advances" make it increasingly possible to live independently of nature. Our buildings are climate controlled, heated in winter and air conditioned in summer. When not inside buildings we travel in movable environments called automobiles and airplanes—no longer restricted by the weather or the limitations of human bodies.

Food has become a commodity. I'm reminded of a time I asked one of my sons to pick blueberries for dessert. Wild blueberries thrive on our land, and he diligently went out with basket in hand. After a short period of conscientious picking he returned home with a few berries, certainly not enough for the family. Upon entering the kitchen he declared that picking was difficult, and wondered why we didn't go to the store and buy a whole container of berries. Food no longer grows in soil, but miraculously appears hidden inside pretty clean plastic packages on supermarket shelves.

We live in an era of fast food that is commercially produced with little attention paid to whether that food will appropriately nourish the human body. Appearance is valued over sustenance as food items compete with one another for the purchasing dollar. Dyes are added to enhance appearance. Food is preserved by chemicals in an attempt to prolong shelf life, even though these chemicals are suspected to be carcinogenic. An even greater technological "advance" is the recent radiation of food which is touted to effectively kill all life in the food, thereby promoting even longer shelf life. The shelf may have life, but the food doesn't!

Social demands have become increasingly more complicated and time consuming. As electricity makes it possible to disregard nature's cycle of night and day, we stay awake long past our natural bedtimes, pushing our bodies beyond their limits. We scurry around in climate controlled vehicles on the ground and in the air, constantly running to catch up with time, a never ending race against time. When we aren't rushing from one social obligation to another, we stay inside our climate controlled homes, "turning on" our reliable source of instant gratification—television.

We have developed symptoms from living an unbalanced life, symptoms of chronic jet lag: sleep disorders, stress disorders, immune system disorders. Rather than pay attention to these symptoms, which range from insomnia to chronic listlessness, we cast a deaf ear in the direction of mother nature. We ply ourselves with coffee, coke, cigarettes, aspirin, alcohol, and antacid in order to keep up the fast-paced life—overextending ourselves—enabling ourselves to keep stretching our body's capabilities. When our attempts to self-medicate fail, we rush to doctors who mete out tranquilizers, sleeping pills and blood pressure medication. Some of us land on the operating table seeking respite from bleeding ulcers and blocked arteries. We're caught on a merry-go-round that keeps turning and turning, going faster and faster, taking us further and further away from nature.

Having lost touch with nature, we've become disrespectful of our planet. Society has "progressed" by clear cutting trees. Forests are razed to the floor, demolished. Green is having a harder and harder time keeping up with her job of replenishing air. The earth is getting warmer.

Instead of valuing air, we pollute it. Many of today's cities are surrounded by haze, a fog of pollutants that hovers constantly overhead. We breathe air that is saturated with residues from automobile combustion and factory production—a far cry from its natural state. On some days our radios alert us to the danger of breathing this air. They particularly warn the elderly, and other vulnerable people, that the air pollution factor has reached dangerous proportions. Whenever I hear these dire warnings I wonder what these people are supposed to do. It is impossible to stop breathing. Should we all be wearing oxygen masks?

And we're polluting our earth. Pesticides and herbicides are dumped on the earth. By-products of "civilization," including nuclear waste materials and dangerous chemicals, are "hidden" underground. Residues of carcinogenic substances are appearing in our water supply. Our future survival is threatened.

It's time to listen to all these symptoms, transcend the either/or, and embrace the whole. Even though we readily forget our humble origins, we are one of nature's creatures. Nature is inside of us as well as outside. We need to nurture the earth that replenishes our water and nourishes our food. And we must begin respecting forests that give us the gift of life—air. Whatever happens to our earth becomes part of us.

As part of nature we take part in her cycles. We participate in the cycles of birth and death, creation and destruction—the universal cycles of suns, moons and planets. We are part of this larger whole. And while we may not consciously think about it as we go about our daily happenings, every moment of life is intertwined with nature.

The rhythms of nature pulsate through us, whether or not we tune in to them, listen to them, or feel them. They are part of us—part of our being, part of our being human. The rhythms of our lives are based on the rhythms of nature.

Our earth, our sun, and our moon do a cosmic dance through the universe, and our inner nature keeps time with their movements, their cycles. The cycle of our day is based on the cycle of our earth, for our day is encircled by the sun as it sweeps in to light up our day and then leaves us to the dark of night. If we don't tamper with this cycle by confusing our bodies with other sources of light, they naturally tune into this rhythm, keep time with the sun. Their time is nature's time.

And as the earth journeys around the sun, moving from fall to winter, through spring, and into summer, our inner nature keeps time with the seasons. We turn to cooling fresh fruits and vegetables during summer, and hunger for warm stews and soups during winter. When daylight is short we retreat within to replenish and renew. As days lengthen our energies return and we move outside.

Our well-being is tied to nature. Because of nature's elemental wholeness we too can become whole. We have a choice. Instead of ignoring nature or pushing her away, we can welcome her presence in our world. We can invite her inside—inside our homes, our lives, especially our selves.

It isn't necessary to live in the country to live a more natural lifestyle, closer to nature. Nature pokes her head through cracks in city sidewalks and follows us wherever we go. She even thrives in dilapidated, depressing, dirty city slums. During summer, tenement house fire escapes are often littered with plants, for no matter where we live, or our "socioeconomic status," we can incorporate nature into our lives. We can walk in parks, participate in community gardens, and invite house plants into our homes.

We can live a more natural life by listening to our bodies—respecting our cycles, our rhythms. By taking care of our bodies, we nurture our selves. We can live in accordance with nature, our nature.

Nature is life. She is the air we breathe, the food we eat, the water that quenches our thirst. She is part of us. We are the whole.

Whole

After we moved to Harmony Farm I became enamored with living a natural lifestyle. I consumed books on organic gardening, holistic health, farming, and living on the land. In the process of reading these books I discovered the Nearings.

Scott and Helen Nearing are pioneers of the back to the land movement. They wanted to live according to their beliefs in pacifism, vegetarianism and collectivism, and felt that they could not do so if they remained in the mainstream of society. Looking to live "the good life," they left academia and New York City in the '30s, moving to a farm in the backwoods of Vermont. When this area became too crowded, they again pulled up stakes, and moved to another rural location.

The Nearings created a self-sufficient, healthy life. They did practically everything by hand: clearing land, building houses, establishing organic gardens, creating a pond. Their homes were fashioned from rocks off their land, and held in position with cement mixed in a wheelbarrow. As I read about their life, it seemed romantic, pure, uncontaminated.

The Nearings became my models. Here were two idealists who didn't only talk about their beliefs, pay lip service to them, they enacted them, lived them. I was enchanted with the idea of following in their footsteps.

While my husband wasn't fascinated by the Nearings, he did want to live more responsibly and closer to nature. He yearned for the "good old days" when people lived simpler, less complicated lives. We shared a similar dream.

Living a more natural lifestyle meant conserving resources, becoming socially responsible. This wasn't easy. We made sacrifices, and put up with inconveniences and discomforts, such as turning thermostats down to 55 in parts of the house untouched by the wood stove.

And it was hard, sometimes boring, work. While my husband chopped wood, I spent many hours, month after month, laboriously sewing insulated curtains to cover our windows at night and keep in the heat. We didn't mind the work as it had a purpose, a reason.

We took pride in our increasing ability to live in harmony with the land and eat in tune with the seasons. During summer we selected meals by walking down garden rows rather than supermarket aisles. While winter was more difficult, we managed to supply much of our own food thanks to a modern freezer, a basement, and an old fashioned cold storage room. I was surprised to discover how easily potatoes, beets, and carrots survived through spring in the cold storage room. Garlic, onions, and winter squash seemed perfectly happy sitting in the basement. And when I supplemented these "supplies" with green vegetables from the freezer and home grown sprouts, we were well on our way toward self-sufficient eating.

Each year we added something new and grew closer to our dream. One year we built a cold frame which extended our gardening season and gave us a place for hardening off seedlings. We also broadened our horizons by experimenting with different vegetables. And, as I was still buying grain, we decided to try our hand with wheat.

After doing all the necessary reading, my husband prepared the beds, planted seeds, then weeded, watched and waited. Soon, his efforts paid off, for the wheat was beautiful to behold—a dream come true. It turned a golden brown and shimmered in the sun. When it came time to harvest, we were blessed with a perfectly glorious, dry, sunny day. My husband scythed it down by hand, and I tied bunches together into shocks. We were a team, connecting with nature, with each other, sharing.

At the end of a long, back-breaking day we smugly brought bundles of wheat into the barn to finish drying. Once the wheat was dry, it required flailing and winnowing to separate the chaff from the kernels of wheat. Doing this by hand was a grand production, requiring exorbitant amounts of time and energy. And as we had only a few meager handfuls of wheat to show for all our effort, about enough to make two loaves of bread, we were grateful for the convenience of a store where grain is readily available—so much for total self-sufficiency, purity!

Our dream of living in harmony with nature was becoming a reality, and I continued loving the idea of living a simple, natural life. But we were also part of another world, society—living in it, working in it, enjoying it. While in some ways we kept our two worlds separate, leaving one to enter the other, they also overlapped, and I felt torn between them.

As much as I loved nature, I kept feeling unfaith-

ful, disloyal. I also appreciated the comforts and conveniences of modern life. My food processor was a
blessing in the kitchen, along with the blender, grain
mill, and juicer. And while I savored taking peaceful
walks, I also fancied the feel of driving a high performance car, one that enabled me to feel my way along the
road, sensing each turn. I enjoyed gardening, but it
hadn't replaced going to movies, plays, symphonies,
eating out.

I kept feeling torn, fragmented, pulled in two directions. One of my feet was firmly planted in the
earth, feeling her rhythms, her cycles. My other foot
was speeding along the highways of America, enjoying
extravagant abundance, favoring the straighter, nar-
rower path of logical, mechanistic thinking. I wasn't
comfortable with these disparities and kept thinking
that I had to choose between these different worlds—
that valuing nature meant renouncing culture. I
should be like the Nearings, give it all up, and live a
pure, simple, uncontaminated life devoted to higher
ideals. I was suffering from the social disease of either/
or thinking.

Despite all my reading and learning, I hadn't em-
braced the whole. While nature had been showing me,
trying to teach me, I'd been seeing the parts and over-
looking the whole. It was when I began centering that
the parts started coming together, for I slowly realized
that I didn't want to cut myself off from the various
aspects of my self. My either/or thinking was the cul-
prit to banish from my life, not the machines that made
it easier, enriched it. When I began looking toward
living a whole life, not subtracting from it, I learned
that the process of interconnecting creates wholeness.

Because we live in different worlds, we can have the best of each—the wondrous world of nature as well as our scientifically sophisticated electronics. We don't have to choose between these worlds. And while I prefer living in tune with nature as much as possible, cycling with the rhythms of the day, the seasons, life, this natural orientation is enhanced by modern conveniences and comforts. I aim to live a whole life.

While there is no recipe for living a whole, healthy life, I have been learning about its ingredients. Food is an essential ingredient, for it is the raw material out of which our bodies are fashioned. Whatever enters our mouths is either burned as energy or transformed into our body's building blocks. I believe that we need to ensure that this food is health promoting, that it offers not only the bare essentials of nutrition, but nutrition that nurtures, promotes wellness, and provides the best possible building material.

Whole food, rather than denatured, manufactured or chemicalized food is, in my mind, more likely to provide for our body's needs. I'll therefore select an apple instead of its juice, whole grain cereal instead of white bread, and fresh vegetables instead of vitamin pills. Moreover, I believe that food is our best medicine, for unlike antibiotics and other drugs, it is preventive rather than palliative, builds up rather than tears down, and is homeopathic rather than allopathic.

I consider organically grown food to be safer—for our bodies as well as those of the farmers, for the earth as well as our water supply. And while I'm fortunate to be able to grow much of my own food, organically grown food is available in health food stores, food coops, and some supermarket chains. There are also reputable mail order companies selling organically grown food. I've listed a few in the Appendix.

Other important ingredients, such as relaxation and proper exercise, are mentioned throughout this book. I could probably continue listing many more, for a whole life has many ingredients, many parts. Each part is important, for it contributes something essential to the whole and is an integral aspect of the whole.

Wholes are made of interconnecting, vibrantly alive parts. They're never static, fixed in time and space, but moving, shifting, transforming. The parts themselves are constantly changing, affecting the whole, and being affected by each other as part of the whole. Each ingredient of a whole is itself a whole, a complex balance of intertwined parts that shift and change.

It is the relationship between ingredients that ultimately determines life's completeness, its wholeness. The ingredients need to be balanced within themselves and between each other. No one ingredient can take over, rule, dominate, for then life becomes imbalanced.

The art of living a whole life is one of balancing. And as variety promotes balance, repetitive work is balanced by creative endeavors; work by play, sleep, leisure; drudgery by fun; structure, predictability, and sameness by change, surprise; time with people by time alone; time with family by time with friends, colleagues, strangers; time indoors by time outdoors.

A whole way of life aims towards balance, with the parts forming a harmonious interconnected way of being. While we sometimes swing from one extreme to another, trying to find a balance, moving into the center helps with balancing. Centering involves finding the ever changing point of interconnection in a life that is constantly in motion—shifting, changing, evolving.

We are engaged in the perpetual process of becoming whole human beings. Growth is never ending, and being whole is a process, a way of being. We can never be whole, for we are always in process.

Being whole doesn't mean that we never feel sad, lonely, angry, unhappy, or even despairing, for there are always events in our lives that give cause for these feelings. Being whole is allowing that feeling, when it exists, to have its place as part of the whole—to be part of the self for as long as it needs to be there. It will move on when its ready.

Being whole is a journey—spiraling back and forth between our inner selves and outer manifestations, between centering in our selves and connecting with other people. It involves growing in different directions, developing potentials, and becoming fully human.

Life is always a balancing act, balancing benefits and liabilities of everything we do. Nothing is all good or all bad. Living a natural life isn't all good. Society isn't all bad. They each have something enriching to offer. Culture and nature balance each other, create a whole.

Walk

Walking down the driveway I'm surrounded by sounds of nature. A few birds are chirping, even though most of their relatives have flown south for the winter. The wind is whispering to the barren branches of oaks and playing with pine tree needles. All is calm and peaceful, yet far from quiet. I continue on my walk, a daily ritual to the mailbox, talking with sheep that are enjoying the warmth of the sun in the pasture. They acknowledge my presence with a few "baas" in my direction. My dog accompanies me, seemingly anticipating my every move. How well she knows me, my moods and nonverbal cues.

As I cross the stream that meanders through our land, I recognize that the stream and I are each on a path through life. Though we travel in different circles, this is where our lives intersect and affect each other. Pausing to listen to the gurgling stream, I surrender to the sense of water flowing through my body, and muse about the similarity of blood and water. Living on Harmony Farm has taught me about the relationship between people and nature. Far from being disconnected, we are interrelated aspects of a whole, each affecting the other in an endless spiral of becoming.

Reaching the road I carefully go to the mailbox, ever wary of the danger posed by cars speeding by. Every car contains a person, each taking their own journey. The cars insulate people from one another and from nature. They travel along the road with nary a glance in my direction, or at the stream that they too must cross. Although I'm tempted to point my finger in their direction and bemoan their lack of awareness, I remind myself that I too am affected by forces that separate us from one another, and from nature.

Opening the mailbox I glance inside and smile at the waiting pile of envelopes and magazines. Some are welcome letters from friends and relations, others are items commonly referred to as junk mail. The mailman deposited them earlier in the day and I mentally thank him as I reach in and eagerly retrieve them. I readily admit that this daily package of paper and ink is but one of the advantages of the "civilization" that I was all too ready to decry a mere moment earlier. Mail connects me with the world beyond my driveway, the social world of other people, places and things. I wonder, is it an accident that we call this little packet of social connectedness mail?

Knowing that language has many levels of meaning, I note the similarity between "mail" and "male," and am curious as to whether this similarity reflects an underlying connection between these words. Others have identified the masculine underpinnings of society. Perhaps my social package of mail is associated with the male-ness of society.

Standing by the road, I continue musing about "mail" and "male," remembering that the word "mail" has at least one other meaning. In addition to the packet of letters in my hand, "mail" also refers to the suit of armor worn by warriors in defense of their society. Again, "mail" has a social connection.

A car whizzes by, demanding my attention. As I focus on this manmade vehicle, I cannot help but marvel at the social advances that have been made. We no longer wear our "mail" directly on our bodies, but are now propelled inside this "mail" which rapidly moves us from place to place. Not one to believe in accidental associations, I suspect they reflect the masculine aspects of our social world.

Leaving the road and returning home, I wonder what this all means. Is there meaning behind meaning, the meanings of these words, and the meanings of their meaning? I'm struck with the notion that these societal connections are male. The social road is paved with masculine intentions.

Continuing to meander back along the path, I glance around and re-connect with nature. I am reminded that nature has been associated with the feminine. We readily speak of "mother nature," and "mother earth." Rounding the bend near the barn, I recall that nature's way is that of cycles. In contrast, the road which passes by our property is straight and narrow, society's road. They are worlds apart. And I live at the intersection.

Photograph by Barbara Fortin Bedell

Bibliography

Alonso, A. "Women and Shame." Paper presented at the meeting of the Women's Interest Group of the Massachusetts Psychological Assn. Boston, MA, March, 1988.

Anderson, S. R. & Hopkins, P. *The Feminine Face of God: The Unfolding of the Sacred in Women*. New York: Bantam, 1991.

Arieti, S. *The Intrapsychic Self: Feeling, Cognition, and Creativity in Health and Mental Illness*. New York: Basic Books, 1967.

Belenky, M. F., Clinchy, B. M., Goldberger, N. R., & Tarule, J. M. *Women's Ways of Knowing: The Development of Self, Voice, and Mind*. New York: Basic Books, 1986.

Benson, H. with Klipper, M. Z. *The Relaxation Response*. New York: Avon Books, 1975.

Bernardez, T. "Gender Based Countertransference of Female Therapists in the Psychotherapy of Women," *Women & Therapy: A Feminist Quarterly*, 6 (1&2) 1987, pp. 25-39.

Benjamin, J. "A Desire of One's Own: Psychoanalytic Feminism and Intersubjective Space," *Working Paper #2*. Milwaukee, WI: Center for Twentieth Century Studies, 1985.

Binswanger, L. *Being-in-the-World: Selected Papers of Ludwig Binswanger*. Trans. by J. Needleman. New York: Harper Torchbooks, 1968. (Original work published in 1963.)

Birns, B. "The Mother-Infant Tie: Fifty Years of Theory, Science and Science Fiction," *Work in Progress #21*. Wellesley, MA: Stone Center Working Papers Series, 1985.

Borysenko, J. with Rothstein, L. *Minding the Body, Mending the Mind*. New York: Bantam Books, 1987.

Borysenko, J. *Guilt Is the Teacher, Love Is the Lesson: A Book to Heal You, Heart and Soul*. New York: Warner Books, 1990.

Boss, M. *Psychoanalysis and Daseinsanalysis*. Trans. by L. B. Lefebre. New York: Basic Books, 1963.

Boston Women's Health Collective. *Our Bodies, Ourselves: A Book by and for Women*. 2nd ed. New York: Simon & Schuster, 1976.

Boston Women's Health Collective. *The New Our Bodies, Ourselves*. New York: Touchstone/Simon & Schuster, 1984.

Breuer, J. & Freud, S. "On the Theory of Hysterical Attacks." Ed. by J. Strachey. *Standard Edition of The Complete Psychological Works of Sigmund Freud*. Vol. 1. London: Hogarth Press, 1966, pp. 151-154. (Original work published in 1892.)

Breuer, J. & Freud, S. *Studies on Hysteria*. New York: Avon Books, 1966. (Original work published in 1895.)

Bown, L. M. & Gilligan, C. *Meeting at the Crossroads: Women's Psychology and Girls Development*. Cambridge, MA: Harvard University Press, 1992.

Brown, N. O. *Life against Death: The Psychoanalytical Meaning of History*. New York: Vintage Books, 1950.

Brown, N. O. *Love's Body*. New York: Vintage Books, 1966.

Brownmiller, S. *Against Our Will: Men, Women and Rape*. New York: Simon & Schuster, 1975.

Brownmiller, S. *Femininity*. New York: Fawcett Columbine, 1984.

Cameron, A. *Daughters of Copper Woman*. Vancouver: Press Gang Publishers, 1981.

Campbell, J. "Joseph Campbell on the Great Goddess," *Parabola: Myth and the Quest for Meaning*, V (4) 1980, pp. 74-85.

Capacchione, L. *The Power of Your Other Hand: A Course in Channeling the Inner Wisdom of the Right Brain*. North Hollywood, CA: Newcastle Publishing Co., Inc., 1988.

Chodorow, N. *The Reproduction of Mothering: Psychoanalysis and the Sociology of Gender*. Berkeley: University of California Press, 1978.

Chernin, K. *The Obsession: Reflections on the Tyranny of Slenderness*. New York: Harper & Row, 1981.

Chernin, K. *The Hungry Self: Women, Eating & Identity*. New York: Harper & Row, 1985.

Christ, C. P. & Plaskow, J., Eds. *Womanspirit Rising: A Feminist Reader in Religion*. San Francisco: Harper & Row, 1979.

Cogan, P. "In the Dark of the Moon: A Vision Quest Exploring Native American Views of Menstruation," *Psychological Perspectives*, 22 1990, pp. 94-101.

Cohn, C. "Sex and Death in the Rational World of Defense Intellectuals," *Signs: Journal of Women in Culture and Society*, 12 1987, pp. 687-718.

Coward, R. *Female Desires: How They Are Sought, Bought and Packaged*. New York: Grove Press, 1985.

Cushman, P. "Why the Self Is Empty: Toward a Historically Situated Psychology," *American Psychologist*, 45 1990, pp. 599-611.

De Beauvoir, S. *The Second Sex*. Ed. and trans. by E. M. Parshley. New York: Bantam Books, 1952.

Dinnerstein, D. *The Mermaid and the Minotaur: Sexual Arrangements and Human Malaise*. New York: Harper & Row, 1976.

Duerk, Judith, *Circle of Stones: Woman's Journey to Herself.*
San Diego: LuraMedia, 1989.

Ehrenreich, B. & English, D. *For Her Own Good: 150 Years of
Experts' Advice to Women.* New York: Anchor Books, 1979.

Fischer, L. R. *Linked Lives: Adult Daughters and Their
Mothers.* New York: Harper & Row, 1987.

Franks, V., & Burtle, V., Eds. *Women in Therapy: New Psy-
chotherapies for a Changing Society.* New York: Brunner/
Mazel, 1974.

French, M. *Beyond Power: On Women, Men, and Morals.*
New York: Ballantine Books, 1985.

Freud, S. *On Dreams.* New York: W. W. Norton & Co., 1952.
(Original work published in 1901.)

Freud, S. "The Unconscious." Ed. by J. Strachey. *Standard
Edition of the Complete Psychological Works of Sigmund
Freud.* Vol. 14. London: Hogarth Press, 1957, pp. 166-204.
(Original work published in 1915.)

Freud, S. *The Interpretation of Dreams.* New York: John
Wiley & Sons, 1961. (Original work published in 1900.)

Freud, S. "Screen Memories." Ed. by J. Strachey. *Standard
Edition of the Complete Psychological Works of Sigmund
Freud.* Vol. 3. London: Hogarth Press, 1962, pp. 303-322.
(Original work published in 1899.)

Freud, S. *New Introductory Lectures on Psychoanalysis.* New
York: W. W. Norton & Co., 1965. (Original work published
in 1933.)

Friedan, B. *The Feminine Mystique.* New York: Dell, 1963.

Fromm, E. *The Forgotten Language: An Introduction to the
Understanding of Dreams, Fairy Tales and Myths.* New
York: Grove Press, 1951.

Fukuoka, M. *The One-Straw Revolution: An Introduction to
Natural Farming.* Ed. by L. Korn. Emmaus, PA: Rodale
Press, 1978.

Gardiner, J. K. "Self-Psychology as Feminist Theory," *Signs: Journal of Women in Culture and Society*, 12 1987,

Gilligan, C. *In a Different Voice: Psychological Theory and Women's Development*. Cambridge: Harvard University Press, 1982.

Gimbutas, M. *The Goddesses and Gods of Old Europe: Myths and Cult Images*. Berkeley: University of California Press, 1982.

Gimbutas, M. *The Language of the Goddess*. San Francisco: Harper & Row, 1989.

Gray, E. D., Ed. *Sacred Dimensions of Women's Experience*. Wellesley, MA: Roundtable Press, 1988.

Greenberg, J. R. & Mitchell, S. A. *Object Relations in Psychoanalytic Theory*. Cambridge: Harvard University Press, 1983.

Greer, G. *The Female Eunuch*. New York: McGraw-Hill, 1971.

Griffin, S. *Woman and Nature: The Roaring inside Her*. New York: Harper & Row, 1978.

Griffin, S. *Pornography and Silence: Culture's Revenge against Nature*. New York: Harper & Row, 1981.

Grinnell, G. "Women, Depression and the Global Folie: A New Framework for Therapists," *Women & Therapy: A Feminist Quarterly*, 6 (1&2) 1987, pp. 41-58.

Grove, D. Syllabus and Workbook for *Resolving Traumatic Memories*. Edwardsville, IL: David Grove Seminars, 1987 (1-800-222-4533).

Grove, D. Syllabus and Workbook for *Healing the Wounded Child Within*. Edwardsville, IL: David Grove Seminars, 1988 (1-800-222-4533).

Grove, D. Syllabus and Workbook for *Metaphors To Heal By*. Edwardsville, IL: David Grove Seminars, 1989 (1-800-222-4533).

Grove, D. Syllabus and Workbook for *Resolving Feelings of Anger, Guilt and Shame*. Edwardsville, IL: David Grove Seminars, 1989 (1-800-222-4533).

Grove, D. J. & Panzer, B. I. *Resolving Traumatic Memories: Metaphors and Symbols in Psychotherapy*. New York: Irvington, 1989.

Haddon, G. P. *Body Metaphors: Releasing God-Feminine in Us All*. New York: Crossroad, 1988.

Hare-Mustin, R. T. & Marecek, J. "The Meaning of Difference: Gender Theory, Postmodernism, and Psychology," *American Psychologist*, 43 1988, pp. 455-464.

Harrison, M. *Self-Help for Premenstrual Syndrome: New and Revised*. New York: Random House, 1982.

Herman, J. "Sexual Violence," *Work in Progress #8*. Wellesley, MA: Stone Center Working Papers Series, 1984.

Hillman, J. *The Myth of Analysis: Three Essays in Archetypal Psychology*. New York: Harper Torchbooks, 1972.

Hutchinson, M. G. *Transforming Body Image: Learning to Love the Body you Have*. Freedom, CA: Crossing Press, 1985.

Johnson, S. *Going Out of Our Minds: The Metaphysics of Liberation*. Freedom, CA: Crossing Press, 1987.

Jordan, J. V., Kaplan, A. G., Miller, J. B., Stiver, I. P., & Surrey, J. L. *Women's Growth in Connection: Writings from the Stone Center*. New York: Guilford, 1991.

Kearney-Cooke, A. "Group Treatment of Sexual Abuse among Women with Eating Disorders," *Women & Therapy*, 7 (1) 1988, pp. 5-21.

Lawrence, M., Ed. *Fed Up and Hungry: Women, Oppression & Food*. New York: Peter Bedrick Books, 1987.

Leonard, L. S. *The Wounded Woman: Healing the Father-Daughter Relationship*. Boston: Shambhala, 1982.

Lettvin, M. *Maggie's Woman's Book: Her Personal Plan for Health and Fitness for Women of Every Age*. Boston: Houghton Mifflin, 1980.

Levitan, A. A. & Johnson, J. M. "The Role of Touch in Healing and Hypnotherapy," *American Journal of Clinical Hypnosis*, 28 1986, pp. 218-223.

Lewis, H.B. *Shame and Guilt in Neurosis*. New York: International Universities Press, 1971.

Liss-Levinson, N. "Disorders of Desire: Women, Sex, and Food," *Women & Therapy*, 7 (2/3) 1988, pp. 121-129.

Maccoby, E. E. "Gender and Relationships: A Developmental Account," *American Psychologist*, 45 1990, pp. 513-520.

Mariechild, D. *Mother Wit: A Guide to Healing & Psychic Development*. Rev. Ed. Freedom, CA: Crossing Press, 1981.

Merchant, C. *The Death of Nature: Women, Ecology, and the Scientific Revolution*. San Francisco: Harper & Row, 1980.

Miller, J. B. *Toward a New Psychology of Women*. Boston: Beacon Press, 1976.

Miller, J. B. "What Do We Mean by Relationships?" *Work in Progress #22*. Wellesley, MA: Stone Center Working Papers Series, 1986.

Miller, J. B. "Women and Power," *Women & Therapy: A Feminist Quarterly*, 6 (1&2) 1987a, pp. 1-24.

Miller, J. B. "Women's Psychological Development: Connections, Disconnections, & Violations." Paper presented at the symposium on Learning from Women: Theory & Practice. Boston, April, 1987b.

Nearing, H. & S. *Living the Good Life: How To Live Sanely and Simply in a Troubled World*. Harborside, ME: Social Science Institute, 1954.

Nearing, H. & S. *Continuing the Good Life: Half a Century of Homesteading*. New York: Schocken Books, 1979.

Newhouse, N. R., Ed. *Hers: Through Women's Eyes*. New York: Harper & Row, 1986.

Norwood, V. L. "The Nature of Knowing: Rachel Carson and the American Environment," *Signs: Journal of Women in Culture and Society*, 12 1987, pp. 740-760.

Nye, A. "Woman Clothed with the Sun: Julia Kristeva and the Escape from/to Language," *Signs: Journal of Women in Culture and Society*, 12 1987, pp. 664-686.

Orbach, S. *Fat Is a Feminist Issue: A Self-Help Guide for Compulsive Eaters*. New York: Berkley Books, 1978.

Orbach, S. *Fat Is a Feminist Issue II: A Program to Conquer Compulsive Eating*. New York: Berkley Books, 1982.

Ornish, D. *Dr. Dean Ornish's Program for Reversing Heart Disease: The Only System Scientifically Proven to Reverse Heart Disease without Drugs or Surgery*. New York: Random House, 1990.

Parvati, J. *Hygieia: A Woman's Herbal*. Monroe, UT: Freestone, 1978.

Pelletier, K. R. *Mind as Healer, Mind as Slayer: A Holistic Approach to Preventing Stress Disorders*. New York: Delta/Dell, 1977.

Perera, S. B. *Descent to the Goddess: A Way of Initiation for Women*. Toronto: Inner City Books, 1981.

Person, E. S. "Sexuality as the Mainstay of Identity: Psychoanalytic Perspectives," *Signs: Journal of Women in Culture and Society*, 5 1980, pp. 605-630.

Plant, J., Ed. *Healing the Wounds: The Promise of Ecofeminism*. Philadelphia: New Society Publishers, 1989.

Polivy, J. & Herman, C. P. "Dieting and Binging: A Causal Analysis," *American Psychologist*, 40 1985, pp. 193-201.

Prozan, C. K. "An Integration of Feminist and Psychoanalytic Theory," *Women & Therapy: A Feminist Quarterly*, 6 (1&2) 1987, pp. 59-71.

Rich, A. *Of Woman Born: Motherhood as Experience and Institution*. 10th Anniversary Ed. New York: W. W. Norton, 1986.

Richards, M. C. *Centering: In Pottery, Poetry, and the Person*. Middletown, CT: Wesleyan University Press, 1964.

Roth, G. *Breaking Free from Compulsive Eating*. New York: Signet, 1984.

Sarton, M. *Journal of a Solitude: The Intimate Diary of a Year in the Life of a Creative Woman*. New York: W. W. Norton, 1973.

Schaef, A. W. *Women's Reality: An Emerging Female System in a White Male Society*. Rev. Ed. San Francisco: Harper & Row, 1985.

Schreiber, F. R. *Sybil*. New York: Warner Books, 1973.

Shames, R. & Sterin, C. *Healing with Mind Power*. Emmaus, PA: Rodale Press, 1978.

Shuttle, P. & Redgrove, P. *The Wise Wound: The Myths, Realities, and Meanings of Menstruation*. New York: Grove Press, 1986.

Sichtermann, B. *Femininity: The Politics of the Personal*. Ed. by J. Whitlam and trans. by H. Geyer. Ryan Ed. Minneapolis: University of Minnesota Press, 1986.

Silverman, D. K. "What Are Little Girls Made Of?" *Psychoanalytic Psychology*, 4 1987, pp. 315-334.

Simonton, O. C., Matthews-Simonton, S. & Creighton, J. L. *Getting Well Again: A Step-by-Step, Self-Help Guide to Overcoming Cancer for Patients and Their Families*. New York: Bantam Books, 1978.

Singer, J. *Androgyny: Toward a New Theory of Sexuality*. Garden City, NY: Anchor Books, 1976.

Singer, J. L. "Psychoanalytic Theory in the Context of Contemporary Psychology: The Helen Block Lewis Memorial Address," *Psychoanalytic Psychology*, 5 1988, pp. 95-125.

Stimpson, C. R. & Person, E. S., Eds. *Women: Sex and Sexuality*. Chicago: University of Chicago Press, 1980.

Stone, M. *When God Was a Woman*. San Diego: Harvest/Harcourt Brace Javanovich Books, 1976.

Starhawk. *The Spiral Dance: A Rebirth of the Ancient Religion of the Great Goddess*. San Francisco: Harper & Row, 1979.

Starhawk. *Dreaming the Dark: Magic, Sex & Politics*. Boston: Beacon Press, 1982.

Suleiman, S. R., Ed. *The Female Body in Western Culture: Contemporary Perspectives*. Cambridge: Harvard University Press, 1985.

Sullivan, H. S. *Conceptions of Modern Psychiatry*. New York: W. W. Norton, 1940.

Sullivan, H. S. *The Interpersonal Theory of Psychiatry*. New York: W. W. Norton, 1953.

Sullivan, H. S. *The Psychiatric Interview*. New York: W. W. Norton, 1954.

Swift, C. F. "Women and Violence: Breaking the Connection," *Work in Progress #27*. Wellesley, MA: Stone Center Working Papers Series, 1987.

Thomas, S. & Tetrault, J. *Country Women: A Handbook for the New Farmer*. Garden City, N.Y.: Anchor Books, 1976.

Tompkins, P. & Bird, C. *The Secret Life of Plants*. New York: Harper & Row, 1973.

Torem, M. S. "Dissociative States Presenting as an Eating Disorder," *American Journal of Clinical Hypnosis*, 29 1986, pp. 137-142.

Tronto, J.C. "Beyond Gender Difference to a Theory of Care," *Signs: Journal of Women in Culture and Society*, 12 1987, pp. 644-663.

Verbrugge, L. M. & Steiner, R. P. "Prescribing Drugs to Men and Women," *Health Psychology*, 4 1985, pp. 79-98.

Walker, B. G. *The Woman's Encyclopedia of Myths and Secrets*. San Francisco: Harper & Row, 1983.

Walker, B. G. *The Crone: Woman of Age, Wisdom, and Power*. San Francisco: Harper & Row, 1985.

Walker, B. G. *The Woman's Dictionary of Symbols and Sacred Objects*. San Francisco: Harper & Row, 1988.

Wallace, D. B. "Secret Gardens and Other Symbols of Gender in Literature: Symbolic Processes in the Creation and Interpretation of Art Works." Symposium conducted at the meeting of the American Psychological Association, Washington, D.C. 1986.

Walsh, M.R., Ed. *The Psychology of Women: Ongoing Debates*. New Haven: Yale University Press, 1987.

Washbourn, P. *Becoming Woman: The Quest for Wholeness in Female Experience*. San Francisco: Harper & Row, 1977.

Weed, S. S. *The Wise Woman Herbal: Healing Wise*. Woodstock, NY: Ash Tree Publishing, 1989.

Woodman, M. *The Owl Was a Baker's Daughter: Obesity, Anorexia Nervosa and the Repressed Feminine*. Toronto: Inner City Books, 1980.

Woodman, M. *Addiction to Perfection: The Still Unravished Bride*. Toronto: Inner City Books, 1982.

Woodman, M. *The Pregnant Virgin: A Process of Psychological Transformation*. Toronto: Inner City Books, 1985.

Resources

Mail Order Sources for Organically Grown Food
  Fiddler's Green Farm
  Belfast, ME 04915
  (207) 338-3568

  Walnut Acres
  Penns Creek, PA 17862
  1-800-433-3998

Americans for Safe Food publishes a list of organic food mail-order suppliers who sell directly to consumers. They also publish the "Safe Food Gazette" and the "Nutrition Action Newsletter." Their address is:
  Americans for Safe Food
  Center for Science in the Public Interest
  1501 16 Street, NW Washington, DC 20036

Organic Farming and Gardening organizations also publish lists of certified growers.

In New England the organization to contact is:
  Natural Organic Farmers Association
  RFD #2, Sheldon Road
  Barre, MA 01005
The contact person is Julie Rawson
(508) 355-2853

In California:
  California Certified Organic Farmers
  PO Box 8136
  Santa Cruz, CA 95061-8136

Index

140, 142, 145, 157, 161,
199, 203
war, 55, 56, 57, 58, 59, 60, 64,
65, 68, 75, 77, 89, 90
weight, 56, 58, 72, 99, 101,
103, 122, 156
whole, 7, 10, 13, 14, 15, 18,
75, 92, 124, 137, 146,
159, 172, 173, 178, 180,
187, 189, 190, 193, 194,
195, 199, 200, 201, 202,
203
wise women, 133, 137, 146

Woman's Voice, 8, 9, 12, 14,
15, 19, 20, 84, 85, 93,
102, 103, 104, 116, 123,
124, 127, 138, 143, 144,
145, 146, 147, 178, 181
women's group, 93, 94
writing, 106, 107, 112, 113,
114, 116, 117, 121, 123,
139

Y

yoga, 30, 31, 34, 142, 160, 161

STAY IN TOUCH

On the following pages you will find books available on related subjects. Your book dealer stocks most and will stock new titles in the Llewellyn series as they become available. We urge your patronage.

To obtain our full catalog, to keep informed about new titles as they are released and to benefit from informative articles and helpful news, you are invited to write for our bimonthly news magazine/catalog, *Llewellyn's New Worlds of Mind and Spirit*. A sample copy is free, and it will continue coming to you at no cost as long as you are an active mail customer. Or you may subscribe for just $10.00 in the U.S.A. and Canada ($20.00 overseas, first class mail). Many bookstores also have *New Worlds* available to their customers. Ask for it.

Llewellyn's New Worlds of Mind and Spirit
P.O. Box 64383-667, St. Paul, MN 55164-0383, U.S.A.
* * *

TO ORDER BOOKS AND TAPES

If your book dealer does not have the books described, you may order them directly from the publisher by sending full price in U.S. funds, plus $3.00 for postage and handling for orders *under* $10.00; $4.00 for orders *over* $10.00. There are no postage and handling charges for orders over $50.00. Postage and handling rates are subject to change. We ship UPS whenever possible. Delivery guaranteed. Provide your street address as UPS does not deliver to P.O. Boxes. UPS to Canada requires a $50.00 minimum order. Allow 4-6 weeks for delivery. Orders outside the U.S.A. and Canada: Airmail—add retail price of book; add $5.00 for each non-book item (tapes, etc.); add $1.00 per item for surface mail.

FOR GROUP STUDY AND PURCHASE

Because there is a great deal of interest in group discussion and study of the subject matter of this book, we offer a special quantity price to group leaders or agents. Our Special Quantity Price for a minimum order of five copies of *Healing the Feminine* is $36.00 cash-with-order. This price includes postage and handling within the United States. Minnesota residents must add 6.5% sales tax. For additional quantities, please order in multiples of five. For Canadian and foreign orders, add postage and handling charges as above. Credit card (VISA, MasterCard, American Express) orders are accepted. Charge card orders only may be phoned in free within the U.S.A. or Canada by dialing 1-800-THE-MOON. For customer service, call 1-612-291-1970. Mail orders to:

LLEWELLYN PUBLICATIONS
P.O. Box 64383-667, St. Paul, MN 55164-0383, U.S.A.

THE BOOK OF GODDESSES & HEROINES
by Patricia Monaghan
The Book of Goddesses & Heroines is a historical landmark, a must for everyone interested in Goddesses and Goddess worship. It is not an effort to trivialize the beliefs of matriarchal cultures. It is not a collection of Goddess descriptions penned by biased male historians throughout the ages. It is the complete, non-biased account of Goddesses of every cultural and geographic area, including African, Japanese, Korean, Persian, Australian, Pacific, Latin American, British, Irish, Scottish, Welsh, Chinese, Greek, Icelandic, Italian, Finnish, German, Scandinavian, Indian, Tibetan, Mesopotamian, North American, Semitic and Slavic Goddesses!

Unlike some of the male historians before her, Patricia Monaghan eliminates as much bias as possible from her Goddess stories. Envisioning herself as a woman who might have revered each of these Goddesses, she has done away with language that referred to the deities in relation to their male counterparts, as well as with culturally relative terms such as "married" or "fertility cult." The beliefs of the cultures and the attributes of the Goddesses have been left intact.

Plus, this book has a new, complete index. If you are more concerned about finding a Goddess of war than you are a Goddess of a given country, this index will lead you to the right page. This is especially useful for anyone seeking to do Goddess rituals. Your work will be twice as efficient and effective with this detailed and easy-to-use book.
0-87542-573-9, 421 pgs., 6 x 9, illus. **$17.95**

THE COMPLETE HANDBOOK OF NATURAL HEALING
by Marcia Starck
Now, all the information that has been uncovered during the holistic health movement is compiled in this one volume in a concise and usable format. With this book you will acquaint yourself with the variety of natural therapies available as well as heal yourself and your family of most ailments.

Designed to function as a home reference guide (yet enjoyable and interesting enough to be read straight through), *The Complete Handbook of Natural Healing* addresses all natural healing modalities in use today.

In addition, a section of 44 specific ailments, including their physiological and psychological descriptions, outlines all natural treatments for everything from insect bites to varicose veins to AIDS.
0-87542-742-1, 416 pgs., 6 x 9 **$12.95**